CHILDREN'S DISCIPLESHIP SERIES | BOOK 2

Discovering Our Awesome God

Bill Bright
Joette Whims and Melody Hunskor

NewLife
PUBLICATIONS

Discovering Our Awesome God
Children's Discipleship Series, Book 2

Published by
New*Life* Publications
A ministry of Campus Crusade for Christ
P.O. Box 620877
Orlando, FL 32862-0877

Edited by Lynn Copeland
Design and production by Genesis Group
Illustrations by Bruce Day
Cover by David Marty Design

Printed in the United States of America

ISBN 1-56399-152-7

Unless indicated otherwise, Scripture quotations are from the *New International Version,* © 1973, 1978, 1984 by the International Bible Society. Published by Zondervan Bible Publishers, Grand Rapids, Michigan.

Scripture quotations designated TLB are from *The Living Bible,* © 1971 by Tyndale House Publishers, Inc., Wheaton, Illinois.

Scripture quotations designated NLT are from the *New Living Translation,* © 1996 by Tyndale House Publishers, Inc., Wheaton, Illinois.

Scripture quotations designated KJV are from the *King James Version.*

For more information, write:
Campus Crusade for Christ International—100 Lake Hart Drive, Orlando, FL 32832, USA
L.I.F.E., Campus Crusade for Christ—P.O. Box 40, Flemington Markets, 2129, Australia
Campus Crusade for Christ of Canada—Box 529, Sumas, WA 98295
Campus Crusade for Christ—Fairgate House, King's Road, Tyseley, Birmingham, B11 2AA
    United Kingdom
Lay Institute for Evangelism, Campus Crusade for Christ—P.O. Box 8786, Auckland, 1035
    New Zealand
Campus Crusade for Christ—9 Lock Road #3-03, PacCan Centre, Singapore
Great Commission Movement of Nigeria—P.O. Box 500, Jos, Plateau State, Nigeria, West
    Africa

Contents

Why a Discipleship Series for Children?

Our children are our greatest assets. In God's eyes, they are a heritage and a reward (Psalm 127:3). Whether you are a parent or a children's teacher, these preteens are the most vital resource you will ever have the privilege to touch.

Proverbs gives us the promise I am sure you have heard many times, "Train a child in the way he should go, and when he is old he will not turn from it" (22:6). What is God's method of training children? It is not to sit the child down and merely lecture him. God's method is a teach-as-you-go process. Before the Israelites entered the Promised Land, God instructed them how to teach their children His Word:

> Hear, O Israel! The LORD is our God, the LORD alone. And you must love the LORD your God with all your heart, all your soul, and all your strength. And you must commit yourselves wholeheartedly to these commands I am giving you today. Repeat them again and again to your children. Talk about them when you are at home and when you are away on a journey, when you are lying down and when you are getting up again. Tie them to your hands as a reminder, and wear them on your forehead. Write them on the doorposts of your house and on your gates (Deuteronomy 6:4–9, NLT).

The biblical pattern for learning is twofold: (1) children learn by watching, so adults must practice what they teach their children, by committing themselves wholeheartedly to God's commands; and (2) children learn by doing, by walking alongside a godly adult who lovingly and consistently guides them. This kind of teaching is deeply rooted in God's Word.

Children do best with active learning methods. The active learning method is basically what Jesus used in discipling His followers while He lived on this earth. Jesus not only preached to the crowds and taught through stories, He also emphasized all the truths He taught through example. The disciples saw how their Master patiently responded even when He was hungry and tired. They watched Him tenderly minister as the crowds pushed and shoved around Him. Their troubled hearts were soothed by His compassion, and their wrong attitudes received His gentle rebuke. They learned through situations they could see and touch, such as distributing the miraculously multiplied loaves of bread, experiencing a roaring sea become calm, and watching the diseased become whole. This was so much more effective for them than if they had simply heard Jesus say, "I can do anything." In the most moving demonstration of God's love, the disciples witnessed the horror of the crucifixion, which magnified the triumph and joy of the resurrection. Whatever Jesus taught, He lived and demonstrated to His disciples.

The Beginnings of the Series

Preteens are at a vulnerable time in their lives. They are changing rapidly. Your 9- and 10-year-old students may still regard you as a hero, whereas your 11- and 12-year-olds may question your authority. But this age is still relatively peaceful compared to the physical, emotional, and mental tumult these children will experience during their teen years. The preteen years are a marvelous time to give children a foundation in God's Word that they can use as they develop into adults.

The lessons in this book will help you harness the curiosity your students have about life. Your students are still young enough to enjoy the activities, but old enough to begin grasping some of the deeper and more abstract concepts of the Christian life.

The adult version of this material, *Ten Basic Steps Toward Christian Maturity*, has been used successfully around the world. The development of the Bible study series was a product of necessity. As the ministry of Campus Crusade for Christ expanded from the UCLA campus to scores of campuses across America, thousands of students committed their lives to Christ—several hundred on a single campus. A resource was needed to help them grow in their newfound faith.

In 1955, I asked several of my fellow staff to assist me in preparing Bible studies that would encourage both evangelism and spiritual growth in new believers. These studies would stimulate individuals and groups to explore the depths and riches of God's Word. *Ten Basic Steps Toward Christian Maturity* was the fruit of our combined labor.

Over the years since then, many believers have expressed a desire to teach these same biblical principles to their children. Some even adapted the adult version to do just that. They found that the basic principles taught in the adult series translated well to 9- to 12-year-olds.

Of course, discipling children is much different than teaching adults. You cannot sit children down with a Bible and lead a Bible study with them. Children need hands-on activities that will help them comprehend biblical principles. They need concrete examples and specific directions on how to apply the teachings to their life. This discipleship series was designed with their needs in mind.

How to Use the Series

This series of four books presents the basic doctrines and teachings of God's Word in a format that will attract your upper-elementary students. The books in this series can be used in two ways:

1. If you are going through the complete series, your students will begin with the previous book, *Beginning the Christian Adventure,* in which they will learn who Jesus is and how they can experience the life that Jesus has provided for each believer. The succeeding three books will teach:

   - *Discovering Our Awesome God*—Who God is and how He relates to us through His Holy Spirit

- *Growing in God's Word*—A basic overview of the Bible and how to study it for Christian growth

- *Building an Active Faith*—How to grow as a believer, including the importance of giving our whole selves to God, witnessing of His work in our life, and obeying Him

Each book will cover one-quarter of the year, and the complete series provides 52 lessons. By completing all four books, your students will have a well-rounded view of the Christian life.

2. Each book in the series is also designed to be used on its own. If you are not going on to the other three books, you will find that the units are complete in themselves.

This book includes a lesson for the children's video *The Story of Jesus,* which you can use as an optional lesson if desired. (See the Resources at the end of this book for information on ordering *The Story of Jesus* video.) The video is an adaptation of the *JESUS* film, an evangelistic tool that has been used around the world to introduce millions to Jesus.

I pray that these lessons will help you touch many children's lives for our Lord Jesus Christ. My prayer is that the upcoming generation will truly change our world for Christ!

How to Use the Lessons

Each lesson in this book is carefully crafted for an optimal learning experience. The lessons are built around several central themes:

- The *book objective* gives the overall purpose for the thirteen lessons.

- The *unit objective* defines how the unit will fit into the book's goal.

- The *lesson objective* shows what the learner will discover about God's message to us within the parameters of the book and unit goals.

- The *lesson application* describes what the learner should be able to do by the end of the lesson.

To accomplish the objectives and application, each lesson contains seven activities. Each builds on the previous activity to move the student to the application. Although the components may appear in different order, each lesson contains the following:

 Opening Activity: Usually a more active part of the lesson, this activity will grab your students' attention and help them begin focusing on the upcoming lesson objective.

 Bible Story: This story or Bible truth illustrates the main principle of the lesson. The story is presented in a way that will hold the attention of your students and engage them in the learning process. The Bible story develops the lesson objective.

 Lesson Activity: This hands-on activity involves the students in discovering more about the truths presented in the Bible story. The activity helps students begin applying biblical truths to their daily life.

 Check for Understanding: This is a short review of what the students learned, to help you assess their progress and what you might need to re-emphasize.

 Memory Verse Activity: This fun activity will help your students memorize the central Bible verse of the lesson.

 Application: This lesson component will challenge your students to apply what they have learned to specific situations in their lives. The application is directly related to the lesson objective.

 Weekly Assignment: Because the purpose of this series is discipleship, the concluding component of the lesson will encourage students to use the lesson application during the week to help them begin developing biblical spiritual habits. At the beginning of the succeeding lesson, the students will discuss how they completed the weekly assignment.

Try to enlist the aid of the parents by explaining about the weekly assignments and what they will do for each child. If possible, explain this when the parents come to drop off or pick up the student, or call them after the first lesson. Some children without a good support system at home may find it difficult to follow through on the weekly assignments. If you have students who do not have support at home, consider meeting with them individually to encourage them and help them grow spiritually. They will also benefit from hearing about other students' experiences. Therefore, make your first activity of the lesson a discussion time about the weekly assignment.

Lesson Structure

The lessons are written to include about an hour's worth of activities. However, you can adapt the material to an hour and fifteen minutes or an hour and a half.

The point of these lesson segments is not to slavishly follow the suggestions given for you. Adapt the lessons to your teaching style without changing the purpose for each component.

The most important aspect of active learning is the debriefing portion of each activity. This debriefing usually involves discussion questions that relate the activity to Scripture and to the lesson objective. Therefore, it is essential to allow enough time during each lesson segment to talk about the activity. If you find that the activities are taking longer than the allotted time, it is better to shorten a later activity than to skip the debriefing questions. If your activities are running short, add questions such as these:

- What will you do differently this week because of what you learned today?

- What feelings did you have during our activity? Why did you have this reaction?

- What was the most important thing you learned? Why was it the most important to you?

- How was the experience of the person in the Bible story like experiences we might have today? How would you have reacted in a similar situation?

As you teach, encourage your students to be risk-takers in what they express. This will require that you treat each person's response with respect. It will also involve listening to what your students say and allowing plenty of time for responses. During this time, assess where your students are spiritually regarding the point of the activity. This discussion will also give you opportunities to talk over many important matters with your students. You may be the only person who can give some students a biblical perspective on life issues. Their responses will help you direct the remainder of the lesson to fit your students' needs.

Most of the debriefing questions are open-ended and require thoughtful answers. Provided after the questions are responses your students are likely to give. If the students' answers seem off-track, help refocus the discussion by restating the question in different words or suggesting a more appropriate response.

The lessons use these conventions to help you follow the lesson structure:

Bold text: instructions to the teacher

Normal text: guided conversation for teaching

- Bulleted questions: questions for classroom discussion

(Italic text in parentheses): possible answers to questions

Gathering Supplies

The Lesson Plan at the beginning of each lesson lists the supplies you will need. Many are items found in typical church classrooms. The lessons assume that the classroom will have a chalkboard and chalk.

Be sure to read and prepare the lesson thoroughly. Some activities may require prior preparation.

Make sure each student has a Bible of his or her own. Encourage students to look up the Bible story as you tell it and to find the memory verse reference. Ask students to read short passages used in the activities, but avoid calling on children to read whose reading skills lag behind others in the group. If you have nonreaders, pair these students with good readers when doing reading activities.

The following rule is essential to keep in mind when teaching children: *The lessons are for the students, not the students for the lessons.* Make sure your students are your priority, not getting through the lesson in a certain way. And have fun learning together!

The Exciting World of the 9- to 12-Year-Old

In some ways, your students live in a world of their own. As teachers, we can never fully understand what they are going through or how they think. But our challenge is to understand them as well as we can and use our knowledge to help them grow mentally, emotionally, socially, physically, and most of all, spiritually. Each child is an individual with unique problems and talents. Each will be at a different place in his or her spiritual journey. At the same time, they will all be affected by similar growing and maturing forces and environments. Keep in mind that their lack of maturity in other areas will affect how they grow spiritually.

If you have previously taught children in this age group, you probably understand how much they are developing in all areas of their lives. The following guidelines will help you see where the student is:

Mental Development
- Moving from literal toward abstract thinking
- Increasing concentration length
- Beginning to understand the significance of past and future but still concerned with the here-and-now
- Creative and curious
- Well-developed problem-solving skills
- Able to think critically

Emotional Development
- Alternating between acting responsibly and childishly
- More self-directed and independent
- Sometimes fears bad situations like parents' divorce or being a victim of violence

Social Development
- Peer-oriented but still looks to adults for guidance
- Relates better with same-sex friends
- Likes having one best friend
- May act in socially inappropriate ways
- Enjoys group activities

Physical Development
- Lots of energy
- Girls may be taller and more coordinated than boys

Likes a variety of activities

Is good with fine motor skills

Spiritual Development

Is developing a value system and a conscience

Can put into practice Bible teachings

Has a clear sense of right and wrong, of fair and unfair

Eager to trust Jesus

Able to make choices and follow through

To help your students build a value system based on God's Word, you will have to move them beyond merely acquiring knowledge to applying biblical truths. The learning process includes these five progressive steps:

1. Feeling

2. Knowing

3. Understanding

4. Applying

5. Practicing

Each lesson is set up to explore your students' feelings about the topic, introduce Bible knowledge, help them apply what they learn, and begin practicing the application on a consistent basis. Each component of the lesson is designed to help move your students through the five progressive steps to making the spiritual concepts part of their lives.

As you teach these lessons, enjoy the world of your students. Do the activities with them. Play the games. Memorize the verse. Enter into the excitement of the activities and the joy of discovering our great and wonderful God. Your journey in discipling children can be just as valuable as theirs will be.

Tips for Teaching Your Students

Each teacher has his or her own style that makes a classroom run well. However, a few basic tips can help you utilize your teaching methods in a more effective manner. The following are suggestions you can use to augment your teaching:

- *Get to know your students.* Every child wants to know that the adults in his life are aware of him and his needs. Begin by calling each student by name. Make a prayer list that includes all your students and keep it up-to-date. Keep track of each student's needs, problems, and talents. Treat each child as an individual.

- *Make your classroom a "safe" zone.* Students at this age can be cruel and thoughtless. Learning skills can be difficult for some students. Other students will have a hard time interacting with children their age. You can help by making sure that each child is treated with respect in your classroom. Praise everyone's accomplishments—even if they do not seem very accomplished to you. Compliment a child who has trouble memorizing when he shows progress. Make a game easier for a child who has poor coordination. And make sure no one in your classroom makes unkind remarks about anyone else. Your "safe" classroom will help students open up during discussion times and feel welcome and comfortable.

- *Look for creative ways to use the available space.* Often we use classroom space the same way all the time. Look around your classroom. Could you move furniture to make the activities work better? Is there space in a fellowship hall, a lobby, or outdoors that would work well for games? Is your classroom big enough to divide into sections for different activities? Can you reserve a corner for discussion and decorate it accordingly?

- *Keep the lesson moving.* Children have a short attention span. They will lose interest if you are not prepared or if you use a slow pace. If students get bored with a game or activity, move on to the debriefing questions.

- *Be aware of your students' moods, personalities, and family situations.* Some days, children will bound into your room talking and ready to go. Other days, it will seem as if you cannot get anyone to respond. An incident during the week may affect a student's behavior. For example, a student whose parents have recently separated may be especially withdrawn or unruly. Learn to recognize the behavior that tells you something is wrong with that child. Keep all your students in prayer for all their needs and concerns.

- *Use consistent discipline with your students.* Write your classroom rules on poster board and post them in your classroom. Then follow the rules. Avoid reprimanding any child in the presence of others. Also, teach your students a signal to get their attention. You might flash the lights on and off or raise your hand for silence. Practice the attention-getting signal until your students obey it. Despite your best efforts, your class will probably have at least one student who will test your patience. As a last resort, you may have to remove an unruly child from the room. Before you begin teaching, work out discipline procedures for unruly students with another adult such as your children's department leader or pastor.

- *Use different teaching styles.* Children, like adults, learn best in different ways. Some are visual learners and learn best when they see things. Others are auditory learners and learn best by hearing. Still others are kinesthetic learners who function best by touching. The lessons are geared to use all types of learning styles, but be aware of how each child learns best so you can help all your students get the most out of the lessons.

- *Be open to adjusting your lesson if the moment warrants.* At times, you will find your students especially open to discussing important topics that the lesson does not cover. Take advantage of these moments to talk with them. Sometimes, an activity will fail to go as planned. When that happens, adjust your debriefing questions to facilitate learning even more. For example, if you were doing an activity with a balloon and the balloon popped before you could finish, you might turn your lesson into an example of how to react when things do not go right.

- *Plan for early arrivers.* Some students will arrive early. Be prepared with activities they can do. One suggestion is to make an ongoing bulletin board that relates to the lesson. For example, Lesson 1 begins with a jellybean activity. Use that theme for a bulletin board. Cut large jellybean shapes out of brightly colored paper and make them available for students as they arrive. Have students write or draw things they appreciate about God, have learned about His character, or notice about God's creation. The students can put their "jelly beans" on the bulletin board. At some point during the unit, talk about what your students wrote and drew, and thank God for all the wonderful qualities He has.

  You might ask students to arrange chairs, set out supplies, or work on an activity sheet that corresponds with the lesson theme. Another idea is to cut the backs off used greeting cards and have students use the lovely pictures on the front to create thank-you cards to God. They can write poems or heartfelt sentences, or even draw things they are thankful for on the back of the pictures. Put the cards in a basket and use them to thank God as a group.

- *Use "after class" moments wisely.* Most of your students will be anxious to leave once the lesson is over. Elementary students tend to begin anticipating the next event before the current one ends. But occasionally a student will hang back. Some students enjoy relating to a teacher and may frequently stay behind. Other students may have parents who are involved in other ministries in your church and have been asked to remain in the classroom until they can be picked up. Rather than resenting the extra time children spend in your classroom, plan for these possibilities.

Allow students to help you straighten up the classroom and begin preparing for the next lesson. They could gather supplies, help you photocopy handouts, or do simple cutting preparations. While you work, discuss what they learned during the day's activities.

Use this time to develop a deeper relationship with the students who linger behind. Over the course of a few months, you may end up spending extra time with most of your students. Preteens will open up to you more easily if you talk to them naturally while you are working together on a project. Occasionally, a student may hang back out of a desire to talk about a crisis in his or her life. If necessary, ask for help from the staff in your children's department.

Another "after class" idea is to have students help you plan and put on a reception for their parents. This will help you meet the parents and understand them better. This reception will work well either near the beginning or near the end of the unit. Make sure you send home announcements for the two weeks prior to the reception. Since the event is for the parents, plan simple refreshments that either your children's department can provide or that a few volunteers can supply. Present a Certificate of Completion to each student for completing this Bible study.

God bless you as you reach the newest generation for our Lord Jesus Christ!

UNIT ONE

Who Is God?

BOOK OBJECTIVE	To introduce students to God and help them understand His nature.
UNIT OBJECTIVE	To help students discover some of the attributes of God and apply the concepts to their lives.
LESSON 1: God Is So Great!	*Objective:* To help students begin to grasp the splendor of God and the mystery of His triune nature. *Application:* To praise God for His magnificent nature.
LESSON 2: God Can Do Anything!	*Objective:* To help students learn that God is the absolute Ruler of the universe. *Application:* To help students write ways they can ask God to help them in daily life.
LESSON 3: God Is Always Fair!	*Objective:* To help students learn that they can trust God because He is a holy, truthful, and righteous Judge. *Application:* To think of ways they can reflect God's righteous nature in their interaction with others.
LESSON 4: God Loves Me!	*Objective:* To help students discover how much God the Father loves them. *Application:* To plan ways they can show compassion for others in diverse situations.

The ancient scribes who performed the laborious task of copying the Holy Scriptures had a practice that illustrated their respect for God. When they were about to write the name of the Lord, they stopped their work and performed ceremonial washing. Then, with their clothes and body clean, they would take up a new writing utensil and carefully pen God's holy name.

What a contrast their example is to how many people treat God today! God's name has become a swear word, and even those who claim to serve Him often speak His name flippantly and without respect. Many people around us do not know who God is and what He is about. Many people hold very disturbing ideas of how God acts and what He thinks. But if they truly come to understand God's character, they will also understand why complacent or hostile attitudes are such an affront to God.

Our society also teaches these wrong ideas about God to our children. Through television, movies, magazines, and conversations, your students have built a wrong view of God. If they attend public schools, they probably have read atheistic worldviews in their textbooks. Some of your students may even have heard people speak harshly against God and Christians. *Discovering Our Awesome God* is an answer for these young learners about who God is and how they can interact with Him.

God's abilities eclipse anything we could ever think or do. He is infinitely great, and we are so small. When we stand on a beach and gaze out on the ocean, its vastness overwhelms us. Those waves can destroy houses and anything else in their path. Yet God is infinitely more powerful than all the waves in all the earth's oceans—even the super-currents generated by hurricanes and typhoons. The contrast between God's omnipotence and our impotence is beyond our ability to even imagine.

God is also infinitely perfect, and we are so imperfect. He is without any fault, without any blemish, and without any deficiency. In contrast, we have innumerable shortcomings. Compare the sight of the entire countryside covered with the purity of newly fallen snow to the slush of a tiny, dirty, mud puddle. The difference between God's perfection and our imperfection is infinitely greater.

Yet with all His power and perfection, God is supremely committed to His people who are so fickle in their commitment to Him. When we consider the depth of His love for us— the magnitude of the sacrifice He made for us by sending His Son to die for us, the plans and desires He has for our eternal future—and compare that with our natural self-centered tendencies, the contrast is beyond our understanding.

How, then, can anyone teach such a concept to children? Because of their immaturity, they cannot grasp all that an adult can understand. Yet their faith is simpler and they are sometimes more ready to embrace who God is than adults are. They can become excited about their perfect heavenly Father who is committed to them for a lifetime.

This unit will help you take complicated theological concepts about God and simplify them for your students. As you do, explain to them the awe and wonder you feel about our glorious Creator. Describe for them what He has done for you and how much you rely on Him as your eternal Father.

Unit 1 describes the attributes of God and Lesson 4 highlights God's love as the Father sent His Son, Jesus. Unit 2 introduces the students to the one Person of the Trinity with whom they are probably least familiar, the Holy Spirit. If you feel that your students need a more in-depth look at the life of Jesus, an option you may consider is to show *The Story of Jesus for Children* video as a lesson between Units 1 and 2. The video presents the life, death, and resurrection of Jesus Christ and challenges children to receive Him as their Savior. If your students are not familiar with the gospel story or what Jesus has done for them, this is a great way to help them see how much God loves them through His sacrifice of His Son. See the Video Lesson at the back of this book for more information on how to order the video and to conduct the video lesson.

LESSON 1

God Is So Great!

LESSON PLAN

OBJECTIVE: Students will begin to grasp the splendor of God and the mystery of His triune nature.

APPLICATION: Students will learn how to praise God for His magnificent nature.

LESSON PLAN ELEMENT	ACTIVITY	TIME	SUPPLIES
Opening Activity	*Immeasurable Greatness*	7–10	Bible; jelly beans or M&Ms; clear pint- or quart-size jar; photo or drawing of candy-filled jar; cloth to cover jar; small piece of paper for each student; pencils
Bible Story—Exodus 2–3, Moses and the burning bush	*What's in a Name?*	10–15	Bible; green, red, orange, and yellow tissue paper; newsprint or tan butcher paper; glue
Check for Understanding	*Writing in the "Sand"*	5–10	Watercolor markers
Lesson Activity	*Mysterious Fact*	7–10	Ice cube in a ziplock bag for each student; water; glass with ice cubes; cup of water; microwave oven or coffee pot
Application	*God, You Are So Great!*	4–5	
Memory Verse Activity	*How Majestic!*	4–5	Bible; 80 square slips of paper; basket; cellophane tape
Weekly Assignment	*God Sightings*	3–5	"God Sightings" handouts

As the king of Israel, David composed many psalms expressing God's grandeur. In Psalm 145, he writes, "I will meditate about Your glory, splendor, majesty and miracles. Your awe-inspiring deeds shall be on every tongue; I will proclaim Your greatness. Everyone will tell about how good You are, and sing about Your righteousness" (Psalm 145:5–7, TLB).

Many other biblical writers also wrote of God's splendor. In the New Testament, Paul describes Him as "the King eternal, immortal, invisible, the only wise God" (1 Timothy 1:17, KJV).

He is so gloriously incomprehensible that our minds just cannot grasp the whole nature of God. Yet we must find some human way to understand God's personality—at least in part. His infinity, self-existence, eternal nature, and self-sufficiency are beyond measure. Aren't you glad that we can know a God who is so far beyond our abilities? We can have complete confidence in a God who is greater than us and any of our problems.

Through this lesson, your students will discover how magnificent our God is. They will learn about His most important name. As you teach this lesson, express to them your understanding of the awesome nature of God. Emphasize that God is so great that we can only begin to grasp His character and abilities.

LESSON PLAN

OPENING ACTIVITY: Immeasurable Greatness

Before Class: Count the number of jellybeans that you have and put them in the jar. Then either take a photograph or draw a picture of the jar of beans to use in class. Before students arrive, cover the jar with a cloth and set it aside.

When ready to begin, ask:

- What is something you have a hard time understanding? *(Allow for individual responses.)*

- What helped you to get to know more about this thing? *(Allow for individual responses.)*

Today, we'll begin with an activity that shows how important it is to study something to get to know it better. **Give each student a pencil and a piece of paper. Hold up the picture of the jar and its contents.**

On your slip of paper, write "Guess #1." Look at this picture and guess the number of candies in this jar. **If students complain that they can't tell just by looking at the picture, ask them to make the best guess they can. Give students a moment to do this. Then have volunteers call out their guesses.**

- Why is it hard to know the number of candies from looking at this picture? *(We can't see the whole jar. We don't know the real size. We can't tell if the picture is drawn accurately.)*

We can't know accurately because we really can't tell much from this picture. It doesn't help us learn much about what's in the jar.

Take the cloth off the jar and set the jar in front of the students. This is the jar in the picture. Now write "Guess #2" on your paper. Now that you can see the jar, write down how many candies you think are in the jar. You should be able to make a more accurate guess. **Give students a moment to do this. Don't allow them to come up and handle or look closely at the jar. Then have volunteers call out their guesses.**

- What would help you make an even better guess without actually counting the candies? *(Getting closer; measuring; holding the jar in my hand.)*

A closer look helps us understand more. Write "Guess #3" on your paper. I'll ask two students at a time to come up and look at the jar. After you have examined the jar, write your guess on your paper. **Allow pairs of students to come up and briefly look at and handle the jar. Then have everyone sit down. Ask volunteers to call out their guesses. Reveal the number of candies in the jar and announce who made the most accurate guess.**

Optional Activity: Give the jar of candy to the closest guesser and have the student share the candy with the class.

Our God is awesome. You may think that you don't know Him very well. We don't know everything about Him; no one does. But we can learn more about Him by studying what He is like. We can see His splendor, learn His most important name, and begin to understand His personality.

Our activity with the candy jar showed us how important it is to study closely something that we don't understand. God's personality is hard to understand. One way we can discover more about God is by studying the Bible, which contains God's very words to us. Here is a Bible verse that tells about God's splendor or greatness. **Read Psalm 8:1.**

Listen for some of God's greatness in the verses that David wrote in Psalm 145:3–10. **Read these verses.**

- What are some ways that God displays His splendor in these verses? *(His mighty acts; His power; His awesome works; His creation; His love, goodness, and compassion for everyone.)*

God displays His splendor in many ways. He displays it through His creation, His mighty acts in history, and His daily work in our lives. He is so great and awesome that we have a hard time understanding Him. Just like with the candy jar, we will know very little about God if we don't get close to Him. The more time we spend with God, the better we will understand His personality.

One of the first things we want to know about a person we meet is his or her name. What about God? He has several names, and one of His names is His favorite. Do you know what it is? You will find out in our Bible story.

BIBLE STORY: What's in a Name?

Before Class: Make a burning bush out of tissue paper. Roll green sheets into loose balls and glue the balls together to make a round bush (the larger, the better). Next, shape orange, red, and yellow tissue sheets into flames by crumpling together the center of the sheets and fanning the edges. Put glue on the bottom of each flame and tuck between the green tissue balls in the bush. Continue to glue tissue flames onto the bush in random places until the bush looks like it's burning. Lay sheets of newsprint or tan butcher paper on the floor to make desert "sand" for students to sit on while they listen to the story.

Have students sit in a circle either on the "sand" paper or around the edge of it.

Let's pretend that we're in a desert. It's hot and lonely. The only living things you can see are the sheep you are watching. You haven't talked to another person for months. While we're alone in the desert, let's think about who God is.

- What do you think of when you think about God? *(Allow for individual responses.)*

God is so wonderful, no one could ever describe Him. His ways are so above ours that we can never imagine what He is like or how He acts. Then how do we get to know God? We can't know Him unless He makes a way for us to know Him.

- How do you talk to a baby? *(With baby talk.)*

A baby can't understand you unless you communicate in certain ways. We make motions, use simple words, maybe even make funny cooing sounds.

- How do you make your pet understand what you want it to do? *(Allow for individual responses.)*

Pets can't understand what people are saying to them unless their owners train them. Even then, animals can understand only a small part of what we say to them.

Think about God. He is so much more intelligent, wise, and complex than we could ever imagine. We can only get to know Him because He shows Himself to us in ways we can understand. He makes the first move. He comes down to our level. He does this because He created us, loves us, and wants to be our heavenly Father. Because He loves people so much, He has communicated with humans in many different ways.

- What are some ways God communicates with us? *(In the Bible; when we pray.)*

The most important way God communicates with us is through His Word. **Hold up your Bible.** His words are recorded in the Bible. The Bible also tells us other ways God has communicated with people long ago. God talked to a man named Moses in an amazing way.

Tell the following story. When Moses was growing up, he had a pretty good life. He lived in the king's palace in Egypt as an adopted son of the king's daughter. Egyptian kings were called Pharaohs. Moses learned from the best teachers, ate the best food, and wore the best clothes. Everyone knew who Moses was.

But Moses wasn't an Egyptian. He was born an Israelite. And the Israelite people—millions of them—were slaves in Egypt. They worked terribly hard. So, although Moses was having a great time in the palace, the rest of his people were suffering.

One day Moses saw an Egyptian beating an Israelite slave. Moses lost his temper and killed the Egyptian. People found out what Moses had done, so he ran away. Moses, who had lived in the Pharaoh's palace, became a shepherd, caring for smelly sheep in the hot desert.

- Do you think God could be interested in a failure like Moses? *(Never, because he murdered someone. Yes, because God loves all people.)*

Moses had not forgotten about God. As he watched sheep, his rebellious heart was changing into a soft, humble heart. That's the kind of person God can use to do important things. **Place the burning bush in the middle of the circle. Open your Bible to Exodus chapter 3.**

One day, as Moses was watching his sheep near a mountain, he saw a burning bush. That was strange. How did it catch on fire? Even stranger still, it didn't burn up. Have you ever seen a burning bush that wasn't reduced to ashes in minutes? Especially a dry bush in the desert?

Moses said to himself, "I will go over and see this strange sight—why the bush does not burn up." (3:3)

As he got closer, a voice came out of the bush. "Moses! Moses!" (3:4)

- How do you think Moses felt at that moment? *(Scared; surprised.)*

Not knowing what else to say, he said, "Here I am." (3:4)

It was God's voice! God was speaking from the bush. God immediately warned Moses, "Take off your sandals, for the place where you are standing is holy ground." (3:5)

When God speaks to you out of a burning bush, you do what He says! Moses not only took off his shoes, but he also covered his face because he was afraid to look at God.

Let's imagine that we are Moses and do what he did. **Have kids take off their shoes and cover their faces until you get to the next question.**

God told Moses to return to Egypt and lead the Israelites out of slavery. Moses was to lead them to a land God had prepared for them. God would help Moses do everything. That meant that Moses would have to go back and face Pharaoh!

- How do you think Moses was feeling at this moment? *(He was scared. He didn't think he could do the job. He was amazed that God would speak to him.)*

Moses was a failure—a murderer and a lowly shepherd. But he had learned to love God. God knew that.

But Moses was afraid, too. Because he was no one great, he wanted to know what he should tell the people so they would listen to him. He asked God, "Suppose I go to the Israelites and say to them, 'The God of your fathers has sent me to you,' and they ask me, 'What is his name?' Then what shall I tell them?" (3:13)

This is the surprising answer God gave: "I AM WHO I AM. This is what you are to say to the Israelites: 'I AM has sent me to you'" (3:14). I AM is God's most special name.

- What do you think is so special about that name? *(Allow for individual responses.)*

Here is the secret of God's name, I AM: it has no ending. Usually, we say something like, "I am rich" or "I am smart." God is both of those things.

- What else could we put behind I AM that describes God? *(Strong, big, loving, kind.)*

God is everything good—but never anything bad. And He is so much more of these good things that we can't even describe how good He is. Could we ever describe how strong God is? *(No.)* How big God is? *(No.)* How much love God has? *(No.)* That's why God's most important name, I AM, has nothing behind it. Because God is always so much more than anything we could write. He's everything.

I'm sure you've heard the ending of the story about Moses. He went down to Egypt and led the people of Israel out of their slavery. God performed many miracles through Moses. One of these was opening a pathway across the Red Sea so the people could cross over and escape from the Egyptian army.

CHECK FOR UNDERSTANDING: Writing in the "Sand"

> 🍎 *Teaching Tip:* In this activity, students will be writing on the "sand" with markers. You may want to test your "sand" paper by writing on a corner to see if the markers bleed through to the flooring. If so, substitute crayons for markers.

Hand each student a marker. Close your eyes for a moment and think about how great God is. When I say, "Go," use your marker to write on our sand. Write "I AM" and something behind it that describes God's character. For example, you could write, "I AM the most powerful." I'll give you 30 seconds to write as many things as you can.

After a moment, say "Go" and give kids 30 seconds to write. While they are writing, jot down sentences of your own with qualities of God that students may not think of. Then say, "Stop," and ask volunteers to read their lists of I AM sentences. Read yours too.

LESSON ACTIVITY: Mysterious Fact
You may want to do this activity around a table in another part of your room.

God's personality is hard to understand because God is so great and awesome that we can't fully comprehend Him. One aspect we have a hard time understanding is the fact that God is three Persons in one. This truth about God is called the Trinity. Trinity comes from the prefix *tri*, which means three, and the word *unity*, which means combined into one. The fact that God is a Trinity is one of the most important things we can learn about Him.

God's three-in-one nature was first spoken of in Genesis 1:26 when God said, "Let us make man in our image, in our likeness." Why did God say "us" and "our" when He was the only Person at creation? The "us" and "our" in this verse refers to the three different roles of God. We can use water as an example to help us understand the Trinity a little better.

Water comes in three forms. **Give each student an ice cube in a ziplock bag.** Look at the ice cube I have given you. Just as ice is one form of water, so God the Father is one of the Persons of the Trinity. He directs action such as sending Jesus Christ to earth to die for our sins.

Look at your baggie. Do you see liquid in the bottom? That's water in its liquid form. Jesus Christ, God the Son, is another form of the Trinity. He sits at the right hand of God the Father and is head of the worldwide Church.

Put a few ice cubes in a glass to cool the glass. Fill a cup with water and heat the water to near boiling in a microwave oven or coffee pot. Now look at the water I just heated. Do you see the steam coming off the water? Watch as I put a glass over the hot water. Place the cold glass over the steam. See the water droplets forming? Steam is a third form of water, just as the Holy Spirit is the third form of God. He lives within believers, guiding us to the truth and helping us stay away from sin.

Ice, liquid, and steam have different uses, but they are all water. That's like the Trinity. Although God exists in three different forms or Persons, each Person in the Trinity is fully

God. At the same time, God is not three separate Gods, but one. No Person in the Godhead is less important or less powerful. Each Person just has a different role. This is a mysterious fact about God that we can only begin to understand.

APPLICATION: God, You Are So Great!

Have kids sit back on the "sand" paper in the same place they sat earlier. One way we can show God how much we know about His magnificent character is by praising Him. Praising God means telling Him how great He is.

Remember the I AM sentences we wrote on our "sand" paper? Let's use them to praise God.

> *Optional Activity:* To help your students understand more about God's names and His character, photocopy the "Names of God" appendix and use it as a study time during class. Or assign the "Names of God" chart as a Weekly Assignment in addition to the "God Sightings" activity. Then, during the next session, discuss how God's names serve as promises to us about how He will care for us and love us. Encourage your students to identify the name that means the most to them right now and why it is so special. Help the students relate God's names to specific events where God has helped them.

Let's bow in prayer and tell God how much we appreciate His greatness. We'll go around our circle. When your turn comes, pray a simple sentence about an I AM statement you wrote. You might pray, "God, I am so glad that You are all powerful." Or you could pray, "God, You are so wonderful because You know everything there is to know about everything."

Pray around the circle. If you have time, pray around the circle one or more times again. Then shout together as a group, "God, You are so great!"

MEMORY VERSE ACTIVITY: How Majestic!

Psalm 8:1—"O LORD, our Lord, how majestic is Your name in all the earth! You have set Your glory above the heavens."

Write one letter of each word from the verse above on a paper square. Put the squares into a basket or other container. Ask each student to select several squares so they are divided among the class. (For example, since there are 80 letters, if you have 10 students, have each person pick 8 squares.)

The letters you have spell out today's memory verse. I'm going to give you a couple of minutes to get together and see if you can come up with the verse.

Give kids a few minutes to figure out what the verse says by arranging their letters. This activity will be frustrating. Then have students sit in a circle.

I gave you an impossible task. These letters can spell out many words in many different combinations. It would take you a very long time to figure out what the letters spell. That's how it is with God. He is way beyond our total understanding. We can never figure Him out on our own. But we can know Him by reading His Word. The Bible will give us a greater understanding about Him.

Read Psalm 8:1 from the Bible. This is the verse that these letters spell. As I read each word and its letters, raise your hand if you have one of the letters. I will call on you to come up and get a piece of tape and put the letter on the board to make the word. Remember, some letters like "e" occur more than once in the verse. But I will only call on one person to put up the letter for that word.

"O"—Who has an O? Let's put that word on the board.

"Lord"—Who has an L? An O? An R? A D? Let's put up that word.

Continue through the verse using this format. When the verse is complete, add punctuation and the reference. Read the verse together from the board.

- What majestic name of God did we learn about today? *(I AM.)*

- What are some examples of God's majesty? *(Creation; His power; He knows the future.)*

Give students time to practice the verse in pairs or recite it to you individually.

 Optional Activity: Teach your group the chorus *O Lord, How Majestic Is Your Name,* and the hymn *How Great Thou Art.*

WEEKLY ASSIGNMENT: God Sightings

Many times we don't have to actually see a person to know that he or she is nearby.

- What is your favorite food that your mom cooks for you? *(Allow for responses.)*

When you walk into your house and you can smell that food, you know your mom is home even if you don't see her. You know your best friend is around when you see his or her bike in the driveway. In the same way, we know that God is here because He has left evidences of His presence everywhere.

- What are some examples of things that show God is here? *(Stars, grass, animals.)*

Pass out the "God Sightings" handout. On this handout, write or draw things you see this week that let you know that God is here. Include as many as you can. Be ready to explain what you wrote down next week.

Close in prayer, asking God to help your students be more aware of His splendor and His majestic name.

God Sightings

When you see a cat's tracks in the dirt, you know a cat has passed by. If you look at a picture someone painted, you know an artist was at work. When you see a machine working, you know a mechanic built it.

When we look all over our universe, we see evidences that God is here. Write or draw things you see that prove that God is with us. Some examples might be the sun, your baby brother, or a spider's web.

God Can Do Anything!

LESSON PLAN

OBJECTIVE: Students will learn that God is the absolute Ruler of the universe.

APPLICATION: Students will write ways they can ask God to help them in daily life.

LESSON PLAN ELEMENT	ACTIVITY	TIME	SUPPLIES
Opening Activity	*Indescribable Distances*	7–10	String or cord; styrofoam or construction paper sun and earth; tape; small round stickers; pens; ruler; Bibles
Bible Story—Genesis 1 and 2, creation	*Immeasurable Power*	10–15	Bibles; 3 pieces of white paper; marker; black, white, blue, green, yellow, tan, red, and brown pieces of construction paper; stapler
Lesson Activity	*The Real Know-It-All*	7–10	Paper; pencils; Bible
Check for Understanding	*God Is*	3–5	"God Is" handouts; pencils
Memory Verse Activity	*Muddled Memory*	3–5	Bible
Application	*God Helps Me!*	7–10	3 pieces of lined paper; 3 pencils
Weekly Assignment	*Omni-bus Trip*	3–5	"Omni-bus Trip" handouts

We have a Royal King whose majesty and splendor are indescribable. Compared to Him, no other ruler is even a blip on the screen of eternity. He does not need to have ceremony or to drape Himself in grandeur to appear more regal. Jewels and wealth mean nothing to Him. Our sovereign God's throne is in heaven far above the universe.

God reigns so supremely above His creation that we cannot question any of His actions. Whatever God wants to happen will happen; His will cannot be thwarted. God's creative actions set the stage for His sovereignty. He was able to create because He was in absolute control of every particle of material even before He brought it into being. Once He formed something, no matter how simple or complex, He remained in absolute authority.

The concept of God's absolute sovereignty is not easy for kids to understand. They can grasp great power, but they have few good role models of adults who submit to authority or consider God's Word as inviolate. This lesson is designed to help kids understand God's rule over everything and His constant presence in our lives.

As you teach this lesson, emphasize God's power, but temper the lesson with an emphasis on God's intimate knowledge of each person on earth. Bring back into the lesson what your students learned in the previous lesson—that God is majestic and lives in splendor.

LESSON PLAN

OPENING ACTIVITY: Indescribable Distances

Before Class: Cut a 30-foot length of string or cord. Create a representation of the sun using a large yellow styrofoam ball or construction paper circle, and a representation of the earth using a small blue one. Attach them to opposite ends of the string. Stretch the string across your classroom and tape it to walls or furniture. If your room is too small, do this activity in a hallway, or use a 15-foot string and reduce the measurement used in the activity to 3/4".

Discuss the "God Sightings" handout with your students.

Then gather students near the "earth" end of the string. Give each student a round sticker and a pen.

I'm sure many of you have taken trips to faraway places.

- Who has traveled the longest distance? *(Allow students to tell of the faraway places they've visited. Determine who has traveled the longest distance.)*

When we take a long trip, we travel by car, airplane, train, or ship. Traveling by plane, you can go halfway around the world in twenty-four hours!

But none of us have ever traveled in a rocket or space shuttle. A fast rocket can cruise through space at 17,500 miles per hour. Compare that to a car that travels 65 miles per hour. At 17,500 miles per hour, a rocket can travel 420,000 miles a day.

Point to the string you have stretched across the room. Let's say that this string represents the distance from the earth to the sun. This is the earth. **Point to the blue ball.** And this is the sun. **Point to the yellow ball.** Write your initials on your sticker. The sticker will represent a rocket. One at a time, place your sticker at the point that you think represents the distance the rocket would travel from the earth toward the sun in one day if the rocket was traveling 420,000 miles in a day.

Allow time for students to place their stickers. Then take your ruler and measure 1½ inches from the earth to show the correct representation. (If you are using a 15-foot string, reduce the measurement to 3/4".) The distance from the earth is not very far compared to the total distance. The sun is 93 million miles from earth. In fact, it would take a fast rocket more than 220 days to reach the sun. That's over seven months! What an unbelievable trip that would be! Of course, no one could ever fly to the sun because the sun is so hot that the rocket would burn up before it even got close. Yet if a rocket could reach the sun, it would take another 175,000 years to reach the next closest star. And God created this entire expanse!

- Hearing these facts about space, how does that make you feel about God's power? (*He's more powerful than anything. He's the strongest!*)

Read Psalm 19:1. Each night, when the stars come out with a glitter, they remind us of God's power and greatness. **Have students open their Bibles. Read Psalm 33:6–10.**

- According to verses 6 and 9, how did God create the universe? (*He just spoke and it all happened. He used His breath.*)

- What else do these verses say about God's creative power? (*He gathers the water of the seas. Everyone should fear the Lord.*)

We should stand in awe of God when we hear what He can do. That's what verse 8 means when it says to fear Him and revere Him. Listen for more details about His awesome power as we hear the story of creation.

BIBLE STORY: Immeasurable Power

Before Class: With a marker, write the words "omnipotence," "omnipresence," and "omniscience" on separate sheets of white paper.

Point out the creation story in Genesis 1. When God created the universe, He didn't need tools, helpers, or an instruction book. In fact, God is so powerful, He could make a trillion universes bigger than ours in less than a second. And that wouldn't even be difficult for Him. When God created our universe, all He did was speak and what He said instantly happened.

Imagine what was here before God created anything—nothing. Of course, before creation, there wasn't even darkness or the color black. We don't have anything in our world that can represent "nothing" so we can't really imagine what nothing must be like. But God knows. This is how God began His work. Notice that God's Spirit, the Holy Spirit, was involved. **Read Genesis 1:1,2.** As we read the creation story, we'll let different colors represent what God created.

Let's see what God did with "nothing." **Select a good reader with a big voice to be the "voice of God." Give the reader a Bible. Announce "Day 1" and read Genesis 1:3–5, having the reader read the parts God said. Have a student staple up a white and a black piece of paper on the bulletin board to represent light and darkness.**

Announce "Day 2" and read Genesis 1:6–8, having the reader read the part God says. Have a student staple up a blue piece of paper to represent water and sky.

Announce "Day 3" and read Genesis 1:9–13, having the reader read God's part. Have a student staple up a green piece of paper to represent grass, trees, and other growing plants.

Announce "Day 4" and read Genesis 1:14–19, having the reader read God's part. Have a student staple up a yellow piece of paper to represent the sun, moon, and stars.

Announce "Day 5" and read Genesis 1:20–23, having the reader read God's part. Have a student staple up an orange and a blue piece of paper to represent fish and brightly colored birds.

Announce "Day 6" and read Genesis 1:24–27, having the reader read God's part. Have a student staple up a brown piece of paper to represent the animals and a tan piece to represent man.

On the seventh day, God rested. **Read Genesis 2:1–3.** God didn't rest because He was tired. God never gets tired. But He wanted to start a pattern for people to follow. He wants us to set aside one day a week to rest and to honor Him as the Creator.

God can do anything! He is all-powerful. This quality of God's personality is called omnipotence. **Tape the paper that says "omnipotence" on the board.** *Omni* means all or everything; *potence* means power. The two parts of the word together mean all power, or unlimited power.

Because God is omnipotent, He can help us do anything. **Read Philippians 4:13.** The "him" in this verse is Jesus. Jesus is God. He promises to help us do everything God asks us to do.

- How would you describe God's power? *(He is stronger than all the rocket power in the world. He can say one word and the whole world comes into being.)*

- How has God helped you do things in your life? *(When I prayed, He helped me not get mad at my bother. He gave me a great mom who teaches me to do right.)*

Another way God helps us is by being with us all the time. In fact, God is everywhere at once. He is right here with us now. There is no place on earth, in the universe, or outside the universe where God is not there at all times. We can't understand how God could be everywhere at once, but He is. This quality of God is called omnipresence. **Tape the paper that says "omnipresence" on the board.** Do you see our little word "omni" again? *Omni* means all and *presence* means being someplace. So God is in all places at once.

- How do you feel about God's ability to be everywhere at once? *(I'm glad because I know I'm never alone. Sometimes I don't want God to see what I do but I know He's still there.)*

- What are some places where you are really glad God is there with you? *(At night when it's very dark. When I went to a new school for the first time.)*

We have one more "omni" word. **Tape the paper that says "omniscience" on the board.** *Science* means knowledge, so omniscience means that God has all knowledge; He knows everything. There is no teeny, tiny fact that God doesn't know.

- How does the fact that God created everything prove that He also knows everything? *(He had to know a lot to make everything in the world. He understands how everything works, even in outer space.)*

- How does it make you feel when you consider that God knows everything about you? *(It makes me nervous because sometimes I'm not too nice. I'm so glad because I know that nothing I do ever surprises God.)*

Right now, let's think about how wonderful God's omnipotence, omnipresence, and omniscience are.

LESSON ACTIVITY: The Real Know-It-All

Pass out two sheets of paper and a pencil to each student. It is important to keep everything in this writing activity uniform to ensure that student identities are kept secret until you reveal them. Use uniform-size paper and only pencils, not pens.

Think of one thing about yourself that no one in this room knows. Perhaps you once owned an unusual pet, or you have never had a cavity, or you own something valuable. You could think of something as simple as the color of your bedroom walls, a dream you have, or a prize you've won. Make sure that this fact is something you don't mind sharing with the class. Write the fact on one of the sheets of paper I've given you. When you finish writing, hand your paper to me.

Give students a few moments to write. You may have to help some students come up with ideas. When all students have handed in their papers, ask them to take the second piece of paper and number from 1 to the total number of students in your class. Then read the first interesting fact from the pieces of paper the students handed you. Have the students guess who wrote that by writing the person's name beside number 1 on their papers. Continue the process until kids have written a guess for each unusual fact. Then reread the slips, asking each person to identify himself or herself.

- How many of you matched every person in our class with his or her fact? *(No one will have gotten all the answers correct.)*

No one in this room knows everything about any other person in this room. We don't even know ourselves that well. For example, have you ever done something you couldn't believe you actually did?

We learned that God has unlimited power and that He is everywhere at once. But God also knows everything about everything too. That means that He knows everything there is to know about us.

Read Psalm 8:3,4. This verse tells us to think about all the powerful and marvelous works that God has done. And yet He still cares about every child on this earth. Listen while I read Matthew 10:30. **Read the verse.**

Let's imagine that you're going to keep track of every hair on your own head. What a job!

- What problems would you run into? *(There are too many hairs to count. Lots of hairs fall out every day. It would take too much time.)*

Let's imagine that you finally got every hair counted. Then you wash your hair and brush it. Many hairs fall out when you shampoo or brush your hair. You'd have to start all over again counting your hairs. Even then, you'd probably miss little hairs growing in.

- Why is God able to keep track of every hair on the billions of people who are alive today? *(God can do everything. God doesn't have to count hairs because He just knows everything. I don't know how He does it.)*

It might seem kind of silly to think of God keeping track of all those hairs. God doesn't really have to count hairs. His knowledge is perfect. He just knows everything all the time. What the verse is saying is that God considers us so important that He knows every detail of our lives—even to the number of hairs on our heads. But His knowledge about us goes way beyond that. **Read Psalm 139:1–6.**

- What do these verses say God knows about us? *(Our thoughts; our words; everything we do.)*

Let's read a few more verses from Psalm 139. **Read verses 7 through 12.** God is also with us wherever we go.

- How does it make you feel to know that God goes with you everywhere? *(Great! Sometimes it doesn't feel like He's here.)*

Even when we don't feel God's presence, He is here. Now let's read a few more verses from Psalm 139. They will give us some surprising information about how much God cares about us. **Read verses 13–18.**

- How have your ideas about God changed since you learned all these promises from the Bible? *(I'm surprised at how much God knows about me. I never thought about God as being able to know all those little things. I'm glad God loves me so much.)*

CHECK FOR UNDERSTANDING: God Is

Teaching Tip: Since you will be using the "God Is" handout for the next two weeks, collect each student's diagram at the end of this activity. Next week, you can hand out the diagrams rather than photocopying new ones.

Hand out the diagram sheets and pencils, and instruct students to write their names on their handouts. Let's look at what we have learned about who God is.

- Who are the three Persons in the Trinity? *(Father, Son, and Holy Spirit.)*

Write these names on your diagram under "One God—Three Persons."

- What amazing act did God do that we illustrated on our bulletin board? *(He created everything.)*

Look at the small, dark triangle in the middle of the diagram. On the top line, write "Creator." In later lessons, we will find out other roles or jobs God has and write them on the other two lines.

In the role of Creator, we learned that God can do anything—anything at all! He is the absolute ruler of the universe. Right above the dark triangle, you'll see a line. We have a special character trait of God to write on this line. The word is "sovereign." It means a supreme ruler. Write "sovereign" on the line. **Help students spell "sovereign."** In later lessons, we will learn other character traits of God that can go on the other two lines around the dark triangle.

- What are the three qualities of God we learned about today that make Him ruler of the universe? One hint—we learned about them with the "omni" words. *(God is all-powerful, present everywhere, and knows everything.)*

At the top of the larger triangle, you'll see three lines. On these lines, write "all-powerful," "ever-present," and "all-knowing." If you think you can spell the omni words, you can write "omnipotent," omnipresent," and "omniscient" instead.

Give students time to write. Help those who are having difficulty spelling words. Remind students to write their names on their diagrams. Then collect the sheets.

God is so wonderful! Let's learn a Bible verse that will help us remember how glorious and majestic our God is.

MEMORY VERSE ACTIVITY: Muddled Memory

Before Class: Write Psalm 19:1 on the board and cover it up.

Let me read our memory verse for today. It tells us about how much our absolute Ruler has. See if you can find the mistakes that I'll make. **Read this with the error intact.** "Psalm 19:1: '[Superman] declares the glory of God; the skies proclaim the work of his hands.'"

- Did you hear an error in this verse? *(Superman.)*

Let me read it again. See if you can spot the error this time. "[Patty] 19:1: 'The heavens declare the glory of God; the skies proclaim the work of his hands.'"

- What was the error this time? *(Patty.)*

Uncover the verse on the board and read it together. Then cover the verse again and repeat it several more times, replacing different words each time. Use the following suggestions or make up your own:

Glory=gizmo

Work=wrinkles

Hands=hills

Uncover the verse on the board. Have students practice saying the verse to each other. If you choose, have each student repeat the verse to you.

APPLICATION: God Helps Me!

Divide the class into three groups. Give each group a sheet of lined paper and a pencil. Assign each group a letter name (A, B, or C). Have each group select one student as the writer and one as the reader. Ask the writers to print these three titles on their group's paper, leaving enough room under each title to add several entries: "God is all-powerful." "God is everywhere at once." "God knows everything."

When I ring the bell, each group will think of at least one way that God helps us in each of the areas written on your paper. For example, under "God knows everything," you could write, "God will help me learn my math assignment when I ask Him to help." Under "God is all-powerful," you could write, "God can help me get over the flu." Or, under "God is everywhere at once," you could write, "I can talk to God when I am scared after having a nightmare." Put the letter of your group (A, B, or C) beside each sentence you write. Write as many ways as you can before I ring the bell again. When you hear the bell, pass your paper to the group on your right. You will receive a paper from the group on your left. Have the reader in your group read aloud what that group wrote. Then think of different ways God helps us and have your writer record them on this new piece of paper. Don't forget to mark your sentences with the letter of your group. Let's see which group can come up with the most ideas.

Ring the bell and give groups one or two minutes to write. (Adjust the time depending on how fast the groups work. When groups have written a couple of ways, ring the bell. Circulate and help groups who are having difficulty coming up with ideas.) Continue this activity until the papers circulate among the groups and each group receives its own paper back.

Have the reader from each group read the suggestions on their papers, mentioning the group letter for each one. Acknowledge the group that thought of the most ways.

WEEKLY ASSIGNMENT: Omni-bus Trip

Large cities have buses that run throughout the city giving people rides to other places. Have you ever ridden on one of these buses? In some places, the bus is called an omnibus. The "omni" part of the word is supposed to give people the impression that the buses go everywhere in the city, although they will only go to certain places.

Pass out the "*Omni*-bus Trip" handout. God is the only Person who can go everywhere and who is everywhere at once. This handout will help us remember that God goes with us everywhere we go. We really are on an *omni*-bus with God because He is always right beside us. At night, He's there. During school hours, He's there.

This week, record some of the places you go where you're glad that God is with you. Each time you find yourself in a situation in which you are glad God is there, make a mental note of it. The first chance you get, draw the place on your "*Omni*-bus Trip" handout. See if you can fill up all the places on your "*Omni*-bus" map.

Close in prayer, praising God for being omnipotent, omnipresent, and omniscient.

God Is

GOD IS

One God—Three Persons

_____, ____, and _____

_____ — _____

_____

Omni-bus Trip

Everywhere we go, God is with us. There is no place we can go where God doesn't go with us. We can think of our day like a trip, with God always right beside us on our trip. He protects us, guides us, comforts us, loves us.

Just like the big hand that is helping this bus, God is always with us helping us. Draw places you are glad God went with you this week. You might draw a picture of yourself in bed during the dark night. Or you might draw a picture of yourself at the doctor's office getting a shot. See if you can fill up all the places on the map with places God went with you and helped you this week.

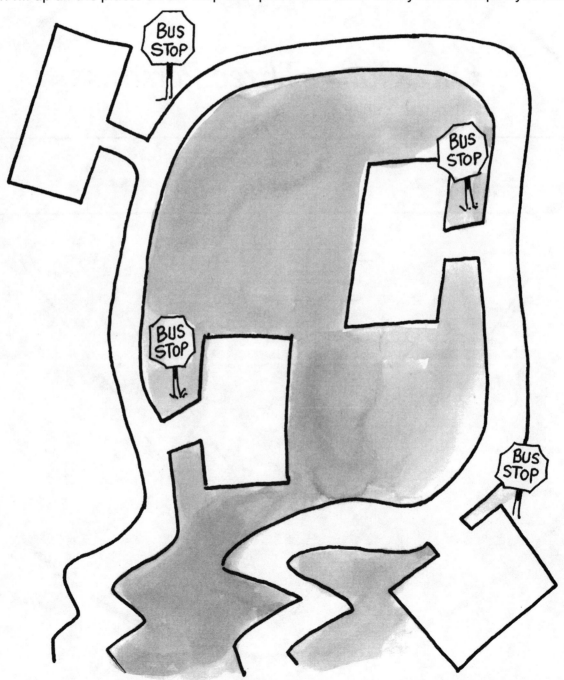

God Is Always Fair!

LESSON PLAN

OBJECTIVE: Students will learn that they can trust God because He is a holy, truthful, and righteous Judge.

APPLICATION: Student will think of ways they can reflect God's righteous nature in their interaction with others.

LESSON PLAN ELEMENT	ACTIVITY	TIME	SUPPLIES
Opening Activity	*That's Not Fair!*	10–15	1 copy of "That's Not Fair!" handout; judge's robe, gavel; scissors
Bible Story—Jonah 1–4, Jonah preaches in Nineveh	*You Be the Judge*	13–15	"Great Gavel" handouts; scissors; pencils; Bible
Check for Understanding	*God Is*	3–5	"God Is" handouts; pencils
Lesson Activity	*Sugar and Dirt*	5–8	Bible; 1 cup sugar; 1 cup dirt; 2 clear glass jars or bowls, one filled with sugar; stirring spoon; slightly soiled white cloth; desk lamp
Application	*Practicing Purity*	2–5	
Memory Verse Activity	*Verse Verdicts*	3–5	Dry-erase marker or chalk; paper; pencils
Weekly Assignment	*Top Ten List*	4–7	"Ten Commandments" handouts; Bibles; pencils

Today, people are less concerned about doing what is right. Instead, they look for ways to cover their tracks, believing that their sin is not that bad or that they will never be caught. They think their excuses and alibis fool God. But, oh, how wrong they are! God told Jeremiah, "I the LORD search the heart and examine the mind, to reward a man according to his conduct, according to what his deeds deserve" (Jeremiah 17:10). We can always count on God to be fair. He will always act according to what is morally upright or good. This is because He is holy, the source of truth, righteous, and just.

Tragically, children pick up the attitudes of adults who say, "I can do whatever I want whenever I want." Your students probably have little concept of authority figures to whom they owe their obedience. Many act disrespectfully toward their parents, lie or cheat in school, and parrot the social line of "I have my rights!"—regardless of how those rights harm others or go against God's holy standards.

At the same time, children naturally understand the concept of fairness. They want to be treated fairly. God has imprinted in their consciences the need for justice for everyone.

Justice is not an external system to which God tries to adhere. He did not have to go to law school to learn how to apply the law. His justice comes from His inner being and is based on His holiness, truthfulness, and righteousness. Moses observed, "Everything He does is just and fair. He is a faithful God who does no wrong; how just and upright He is!" (Deuteronomy 32:4, NLT). God cannot be bribed or corrupted because His judgments are grounded in integrity. Since He has all the facts at His disposal (omniscience and omnipresence), He cannot be fooled. His decisions are always based on absolute truth. And when God pronounces judgment, He has the power to carry out the punishment (omnipotence).

God's standard is the benchmark by which all human behavior is measured. Your students need to grasp the fact that God will not excuse their behavior, but He will forgive them. They need to learn that they can trust God to treat them the same way today, tomorrow, and in the distant future. They should fear the consequences for their sin, but they also need to embrace His love and forgiveness as their heavenly Father.

As you teach this lesson, keep these facts about your students in mind:

1. Many do not have a clear idea of what kinds of sin they may be practicing and the consequences of their sin. They need a stronger sense of the sin in their lives.

2. Many may have a distorted view of God's wrath because of the actions of unjust or untruthful parents or other adults in their lives. They need to see God as truthful and just.

3. Many may fear the future because of what they see as injustice in our society and the world. They need to place their trust in God for their future.

4. Most do not have a concept of holiness. It is a quality of being. God's nature is holy. It cannot be anything else, just as sugar cannot be bitter. God's righteousness is how He acts because He is holy. He always does what is "right."

LESSON PLAN

OPENING ACTIVITY: That's Not Fair!

Before Class: Cut the "That's Not Fair!" handout along the dotted lines. Set up a mini court scene in your classroom. Put a small table with one chair for the judge. In front of the table, set two chairs on the left for the defense and two chairs on the right for the prosecution.

Allow volunteers to share what they drew on their "*Omni*-bus Trip" handout.

Select students to play these parts: judge, defense lawyer, defendant, prosecution, and plaintiff. Have the judge wear the robe. Give him (her) the gavel. Give the prosecutor and the plaintiff the slip of paper labeled "Prosecutor's Arguments"; give the defense lawyer and defendant the one labeled "Defense Arguments"; and give the judge the "Judge's Decision." Have the remaining students sit in rows of chairs to represent the viewers' gallery. Give the defense and the prosecution a few moments to read their arguments. They should follow the numbered points on their slips of paper. The judge should read over the "Judge's Decision." When everything is ready, introduce the case by giving the following information.

In a courtroom, two parties take sides to argue their cases. On one side are the prosecutor and the plaintiff. The plaintiff is the victim of the crime; the prosecutor is the lawyer for the plaintiff. On the other side are the defense lawyer and the defendant. The defendant is the one who is accused of the crime. In many cases, a jury is not used. Instead, the judge decides the case.

These are the facts in the case. Between 1:00 and 2:00 in the afternoon last month, a bike was stolen on Golden Avenue. It was a high-tech mountain bike, and it disappeared out of the plaintiff's front yard. Days later, the defendant was arrested and charged with the crime. Today, the defense and the prosecution will argue the case. After hearing all the evidence, the judge will decide whether the defendant is guilty or not guilty.

Give the prosecution up to three minutes to argue the case. Then give the defense three minutes to argue the case. When they finish, have everyone sit to hear the judge's verdict. Instruct the judge to read the verdict exactly as it is written on the "Judge's Decision." Then discuss the following questions, allowing the courtroom audience to participate.

• Do you think that the judge's decision was fair? Why? *(No, because he didn't look at the facts. He thought of his son first.)*

• What was the judge's decision based on? *(How the defendant looked; how he felt about the defendant; that the lawyer was his son.)*

- Were these the right things to base a decision on? Why? *(No, because looks aren't always right. People should be fair no matter who they know or don't know.)*

- What should the judge have based his decision on? *(The evidence, the facts; the truth.)*

- How did you feel when someone treated you unfairly? *(Allow for individual responses. Encourage students to briefly explain the circumstances.)*

- What are some reasons why a person might treat someone unfairly? *(He doesn't know the facts. She doesn't like that person for some reason. He doesn't understand the problem.)*

We've all treated people unfairly at times. And we've had people treat us unfairly—even good friends. Unfairness is a part of our lives. There is only one person who is completely fair. He is fairer than anyone who has ever lived. That Person is God.

God is the perfect Judge because He is completely fair and because He sees everything, knows everything, and is all-wise. There is nothing He doesn't understand. We can trust God to make the right decisions because He is always fair. Let's look at the story of a real person in the Bible to see how fair God is.

BIBLE STORY: You Be the Judge

Distribute scissors, pencils, and the "Great Gavel" handouts. Have students cut out the gavel and write "fair" on one side and "unfair" on the other. Tell each portion of the story, then ask the question that follows that portion. Give students time to set out their gavels. Count how many "fairs" and "unfairs" you see. Then discuss the students' reasons for their answers. In your discussion, bring out the numbered points that follow that question.

As I tell the story, I will stop and ask a question about what is fair or unfair about the actions in the story. You be the judge. If you think the answer is fair, set the "fair" side of your gavel in front of you. If you think the answer is unfair, put up the "unfair" side of your gavel.

Our story comes from a small book in the Old Testament called Jonah. **Open your Bible to the book of Jonah and show your students.** Jonah was a prophet of God, a person who brought God's message to people.

God told Jonah to go to Nineveh and preach to the people. God had seen that the people were acting very wickedly. He wanted to warn them that if they didn't change their ways, He would destroy their city in forty days.

Jonah didn't want to go to Nineveh. The city was the capital of Assyria, a country that was the enemy of Jonah's people, the Israelites.

- Is it fair that God asked Jonah to drop what he was doing and go to these people?

1. *God has the right to ask us to do anything, because He made us.*

2. *Jonah was a prophet, so in a sense he "worked for God."*

Jonah ran away from God. He went to Joppa, located on the shores of the Mediterranean Sea. He paid for a ticket on a ship going away from Nineveh. He thought he could hide from God.

Once on the ship, Jonah went below the deck and fell asleep. He must have been pretty sure he had escaped God's notice since he felt he could take a few moments out for a nap. While he was sleeping, a huge storm blew in. God sent this storm. The wind and waves were so violent that the sailors thought the ship was going to break into pieces.

The sailors prayed to their gods to save them, but the storm got worse. They had heard that Jonah's God was powerful. They woke Jonah and told him about the situation. Jonah admitted that the storm was his fault. His God, the only true God, was displeased because Jonah had disobeyed. Jonah told the sailors that if they threw him overboard, their ship would be saved.

The sailors didn't want to throw Jonah overboard. They thought Jonah's God would be angry with them if they harmed Jonah. So the sailors threw the ship's cargo overboard. They rowed as hard as they could to reach land. But nothing worked. Finally, out of desperation, they threw Jonah overboard and cried out to God not to punish them for what they had done. The storm suddenly disappeared, so the sailors worshiped the one true God.

- Did God treat the sailors fairly?

1. *Because of the storm sent by God, the sailors saw the power of God and believed in Him.*

2. *God didn't destroy the ship and everyone on it for Jonah's sin.*

God sent a great fish to swallow Jonah. He was in the belly of the fish for three days and three nights. Imagine what that must have been like! But while he was in the fish, Jonah's attitude began to change. He realized that he couldn't hide from God. He told the Lord that he would obey Him. Then the fish spit Jonah onto the shore.

- Was God treating Jonah fairly?

1. *God could have let Jonah drown, but He saved him instead.*

2. *God used the time Jonah spent in the fish to help Jonah become more obedient.*

Jonah went directly to Nineveh. The city was so big that it would take a person three days to walk through it. There were about 600,000 people living in Nineveh at that time. Jonah began warning the people that God was displeased with their wicked deeds. If they didn't repent, or feel sorry about their sins and start acting righteously, God would destroy the city in forty days.

- Would God be fair if He destroyed all those people?

1. *Since God is holy, He cannot let sin go unpunished.*

2. *God gives warnings to people who are doing wrong things. People sometimes choose to ignore God's warnings. Then they suffer the consequences.*

The people repented when they heard Jonah's message. Even the king of Nineveh repented. The people all fasted (stopped eating for a short while) and put on old clothes to show how sorry they were about their sins. They called on God to save their city. When God saw how the people had changed their ways, He had compassion and didn't destroy them.

● Did God treat the people of Nineveh fairly?

1. *He saw their changed attitudes and had compassion on them. He promises to notice when people change their ways.*

2. *God knew before He talked to Jonah that the people would listen to a message from God.*

This story has a happy ending. Jonah obeyed God. The people repented of their sins and worshiped God. The city was saved. But why wasn't Jonah happy?

Jonah was angry because God didn't destroy the people. He went up on a hillside to watch the city. He was thinking something like this: *I told the people that God was going to destroy the city. That was the message God gave me to preach. But now God says He isn't going to do what I said He would do. Think of how that makes me look. And the people of Nineveh have been our enemies for years—they deserve to die. I'm so depressed about my situation that I just want to give up and die!*

● Was Jonah's attitude toward the people of Nineveh fair?

1. *God had been gracious to Jonah and didn't destroy him in the storm when Jonah was running away from God. But now Jonah wants God to destroy other people who also were sinning. Jonah's attitude was selfish.*

2. *Jonah thought more of his own reputation than of the lives of thousands of people in Nineveh.*

While Jonah was feeling depressed, God caused a plant to grow over his head and shade him from the strong heat of the sun. Jonah was happy about that plant.

The next day, God caused a worm to chew on the plant until it died. A hot wind came up that made Jonah feel sick. Jonah was upset because the plant had died.

Then God showed Jonah how unfair his attitude was. He was more concerned about his own comfort than about the lives of 120,000 children in Nineveh.

Who would you rather have in charge: God or Jonah? God is the perfect Judge. His decisions are always right.

A good judge has some qualities that make him a good judge. Let's look at some of the qualities of God that make Him the perfect Judge.

CHECK FOR UNDERSTANDING: God Is

Pass out pencils, and return each student's "God Is" diagram that you collected during the previous lesson. If you have new students, have new "God Is" handouts to give to them and ask them to write their names on their handouts. The "God Is" handouts will

DISCOVERING OUR AWESOME GOD

be used again during the next lesson, so collect each student's diagram at the end of this activity.

Now let's look at what we have learned about God's role as perfect Judge that we can add to our diagram.

Inside the darkest triangle, on the righthand side, have students write "Judge" on the blank line.

- What are some qualities of a good judge? *(He is fair about the sentences he gives to criminals. She takes the time to get all the facts straight. He is wise.)*

Under "Judge" in the lighter triangle, have students write "holy." On the three blank lines at the edge of the triangle, have students write "truthful," "righteous," and "just."

- Of the three qualities that we just wrote on our diagram, which one impresses you most about God? *(Allow for individual responses.)*

- Which quality makes you the most afraid of God? *(Allow for individual responses.)*

It is always hard to come before a judge if you have broken the law. He has the power in his hands. He has the law behind him. That is also true about God. He created the moral laws we live by. He enforces them, too. Everyone who breaks one of God's laws will suffer the consequences.

But God is not only a Judge; He is also our Savior. In the next lesson, we will find out how His role as Savior makes His role as Judge even more special to us. For now, let's think about God's qualities as a judge—His holiness, truthfulness, righteousness, and fairness.

LESSON ACTIVITY: Sugar and Dirt
On a table at the front of your classroom, set out the cups of sugar and dirt, the two glass jars, the white cloth, desk lamp, and spoon. God is the perfect Judge because of His holiness. Let's read Exodus 15:11. **Read verse.** Moses and the Israelite people sang this verse to

God. They were rejoicing over God's holiness. But what is holiness? It means to be completely set apart from sin. Only God is holy. He is pure and righteous. Unlike us, He has never sinned. Let's do a demonstration to help us understand how holy God is.

Hold up the jar filled with sugar. Let's say this pure white sugar represents God's holiness. The sugar is pure and good like God is pure and holy. **Set down the jar of sugar and hold up the empty jar.** Let's say this jar represents your life. **Pour in the cup of sugar.** We all do some good things every day.

● What's one thing you did today that was good and right? *(Allow for responses.)*

But we all do wrong things, too. **Pour a spoonful of dirt into the jar of sugar and stir.** Now this sugar isn't pure anymore. Although it might look good, it has been contaminated with dirt. But we do more than sin just a little. We sin all the time. **Pour the rest of the cup of dirt into the sugar and stir.** The more we sin, the more our sin shows up in our lives.

Would you like to sprinkle this sugar on your cereal tomorrow morning? That wouldn't taste good at all. Actually, the sugar isn't good for anything now. Can anyone come up here and separate the dirt from the sugar? No, no one can.

That's just the way it is with sin. We can't remove the sin from our lives. Our lives are contaminated. Because of our sin, we can never become holy like God.

But what about people who think they only sin a little, so that's okay? Is it okay? Are they holy?

Once there was a man who wore a pure, white suit. One day, he was invited to tour the deepest part of a coal mine. Coal is a hard, black lump dug out of the ground that is used for fuel. Coal leaves a dark, oily dust. Using his flashlight, the man walked around the mineshafts, looking at everything. He was not aware that he was brushing up against the dirty walls of the mine. In the darkness, his suit looked white. But when he resurfaced into the light of the noonday sun, he saw that his white suit had become sooty and dirty.

Dim the lights. Hold up the white cloth. This cloth looks clean in this light. **Turn on the desk lamp and hold the cloth in front of the light. The light will reveal the dirt.** Now we see that the cloth is dirty. That's like us when we look into God's holy Word. His holiness reveals our sins. That's why God's holiness makes Him the perfect Judge. He can recognize all sin. This is a good picture of God's holiness compared to our sinfulness. The bright light or sun is like God's holiness. Just as the light revealed the dirt, God's holiness reveals our sin-stained lives.

APPLICATION: Practicing Purity

God is our perfect Judge because of His holiness. And because He is holy, He is always fair, truthful, and righteous. God's holiness means that He will never tell a lie or even bend the truth. God's holiness also means that He always acts righteously. Let's see if we can find these characteristics of God in the following examples. They will help show us how to put God's attributes or characteristics into our lives. **Read each example and then ask the ques-**

tions. Discuss how each attribute comes from God's nature, that He is completely holy, truthful, righteous, and just. He can be no other way.

EXAMPLE ONE

Do you remember the story of the burning bush? Moses was tending sheep in the desert one day when he saw a burning bush that never burned up! He went over to investigate. When he got close, God called to him from the bush, "Moses, Moses!" Moses said, "Here I am." God said, "Do not come any closer. Take off your sandals, for the place where you are standing is holy ground." Hearing God's voice, Moses hid his face. He couldn't look at God.

- What attribute is described here? *(God's holiness.)*

We can never become holy like God is holy, but God expects us to live a pure life according to His holy standards.

- How can we live pure lives for God? *(Don't watch bad movies or look at bad magazines. Don't say bad things like swear words.)*

EXAMPLE TWO

We can trust God's holy Word. Psalm 119:151,152 says, "All your commands are true. Long ago I learned from your statutes that You established them to last forever." This tells us that every word in the Bible can be trusted to be true.

- What attribute is this? *(God's truthfulness.)*

God is a truthful Judge. Therefore, we can believe what He says and obey His commands.

- How can we be truthful like God is truthful? *(Tell the truth even when it's hard to do it. Make sure we always say what's right.)*

EXAMPLE THREE

God brought Moses to the top of Mount Sinai and gave him the Ten Commandments. They are a set of standards that God expects His people to obey. While Moses was receiving the standards, God's people were disobeying His commands by building an idol. The people were not doing what was right. God was very displeased with them.

- What attribute is this? *(God's righteousness.)*

Because God is a righteous Judge, we should live by His standards and rules.

- In what ways can we live by God's standards and rules? *(We can obey the Ten Commandments. We can love one another because that's God's rule.)*

EXAMPLE FOUR

Earlier, we heard a story about Jonah. God saw that the people of Nineveh were acting sinfully. He sent Jonah to tell them to repent or they would be destroyed. When they repented, God spared them.

- What attribute is this? *(God's justice or fairness.)*

Because God is a just Judge, we know He will always treat us fairly. He expects us to treat others fairly too.

- How can we treat others fairly at school? *(We can let others have a turn. We won't call other people names.)*

Let's learn a verse that will help us remember that God is the Holy One.

MEMORY VERSE ACTIVITY: Verse Verdicts
Write the following on the chalkboard:

a. *Who among the gods is like you, O LORD?*

b. *Who is like you—majestic in holiness,*

c. *awesome in glory,*

d. *working wonders? Exodus 15:11*

Many people put something or someone in God's place in their lives. They consider these things or people as important as God. That is very wrong. Let's think of ways that people do this.

Have the class read the verse in unison. Talk about what each phrase means and how it refers to God. Then split the class into four groups, assigning each one phrase of the memory verse (a, b, c, or d). Give each group paper and a pencil. Ask groups to list three or more things that people substitute for God that goes along with the subject in their phrase. Circulate among groups and help them. The following are ideas:

a. **idols, Mohammed, Buddha**

b. **people who have done great things: Abraham Lincoln, Mother Teresa, the apostle Paul**

c. **riches like golden palaces, the Hope diamond, or dazzling crowns**

d. **people who do amazing feats like Michael Jordan, nuclear scientists, or life-saving doctors**

When groups finish, gather as a class. We are going to give a yes or no verdict for each item that people substitute for God. Together, we will read each phrase of our verse aloud, then the group assigned that phrase will read their list of substitutes. We will answer yes or no to each item.

Example:

The whole class reads, "Who among the gods is like you, O LORD?" Group A answers, "Idols!" The whole class responds, "No!" Repeat for each "wrong" response. Then go through the verse once more, responding, "No one but You, God!" after each phrase.

WEEKLY ASSIGNMENT: Top Ten List

Have you ever heard of the "Top Ten List"? It's a list of the ten most important items concerning a topic. Does God have a Top Ten List? One list would certainly be the Ten Commandments.

Distribute the "Ten Commandments" handout, pencils, and Bibles. Read through the Ten Commandments with your students. Then discuss the ones that apply to them, helping them think of ways they can *obey* the rules, not *disobey* them. Show students where to find the Ten Commandments in the Bible (Exodus 20:1–17).

If these Ten Commandments are on God's Top Ten List, then they should be important to us too. Let's make our own Top Ten List of ways we've followed these commandments this week.

Have students turn over their "Ten Commandments" handouts and number from 1 to 10. Have them label their list the "Top Ten List." This week, each time a student obeys a commandment, he writes it on his Top Ten List along with the date and time. Remind students to bring their Top Ten Lists with them to the next session.

Close in prayer, asking God to help your students keep the Top Ten List this week.

That's Not Fair!

Prosecution Arguments

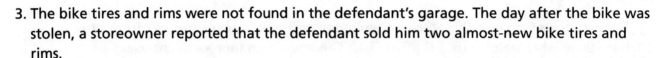

1. Several witnesses saw the defendant near the bike just before it was stolen.

2. The serial number of the stolen bike was found on one of the bike parts laying around the defendant's garage.

3. The bike tires and rims were not found in the defendant's garage. The day after the bike was stolen, a storeowner reported that the defendant sold him two almost-new bike tires and rims.

4. The bike parts in the defendant's garage were the same color as those on the stolen bike.

Defense Arguments

1. The defendant claims he was sleeping in his bedroom at the time the bike was stolen. He had stayed up very late the night before studying for a math test.

2. The bike could not be identified because all the pieces were never put back together.

3. No one saw the defendant put the bike parts in the garage. Someone else could have put them there.

4. A lot of bikes are the same color as the stolen bike.

Judge's Decision

The evidence is strongly against the defendant. It looks like he stole the bike. Witnesses saw him near the bike. The serial number of the stolen bike was on the bike parts found in his garage. The defendant sold bike tires just like the ones on the stolen bike.

On the other hand, the defendant looks like a nice person. Sometimes, he smiles so nicely. He has a lawyer who is dressed in nice clothes. The defense lawyer is my son, and he needs to win this case to get a better reputation as a lawyer. For these reasons, I find the defendant NOT GUILTY of stealing the bike.

Great Gavel

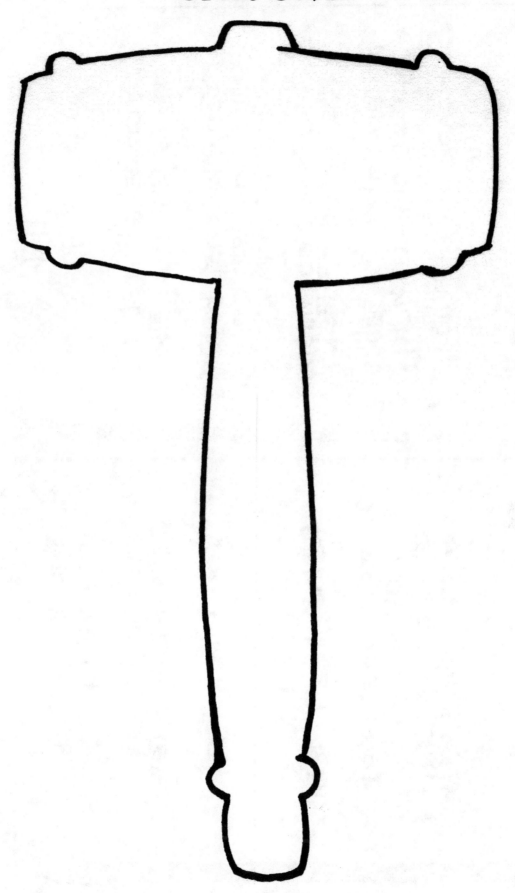

Ten Commandments

1. You shall have no other gods.

2. You shall not make for yourself an idol... You shall not bow down to them or worship them.

3. You shall not misuse the name of the Lord.

4. Remember the Sabbath by keeping it holy.

5. Honor your father and mother.

6. You shall not murder.

7. You shall not commit adultery.

8. You shall not steal.

9. You shall not give false testimony.

10. You shall not covet... anything that is your neighbor's.

God Loves Me!

LESSON PLAN

OBJECTIVE: Students will discover how much God the Father loves them.

APPLICATION: Students will plan ways they can show compassion for others in diverse situations.

LESSON PLAN ELEMENT	ACTIVITY	TIME	SUPPLIES
Opening Activity	*God's Love Bears All*	5–10	2 paper or styrofoam cups; markers; 10 large books; slips of paper; pencils; tape; 2 bricks; Bible
Bible Story—Genesis 22:1–19, Abraham sacrifices Isaac	*Eternal Love*	15–20	Brown paper lunch bags; old newspapers; Bible; masking tape; dry-erase marker or chalk; markers; gospel tracts (optional)
Check for Understanding	*God Is*	3–5	"God Is" handouts; pencils
Lesson Activity	*Caring Tour*	8–10	3 pieces of paper; marker; tape; 1 copy of "Caring Tour" and "Suitcase Stuffings" handouts; scissors; badge (optional); small suitcase; facial tissues; bouquet of artificial flowers; Bible
Memory Verse Activity	*No Barriers*	4–7	12–24 cardboard bricks; dry-erase marker or chalk
Application	*Mercy! Mercy!*	3–5	
Weekly Assignment	*Now On to Real Life*	2–3	"Suitcase Stuffings" handouts; scissors

One of the most devastating phrases a child can hear from his parents is, "I won't love you if you do that." The pain of conditional love is rampant throughout our society. With or without words, our culture communicates conditional love:

"If you're not beautiful, you're not worth as much."
"If you can't excel in sports or academics, no one will like you."
"Unless you have lots of money and things, you aren't important."

What a terrible message to send to little ones who have no control over the way they look, the talents they possess, or the circumstances into which they are born.

Our children need to hear that God's love is unchanging and everlasting. God's sacrifice in planning for our salvation was set in motion in eternity past: "He chose us in Him before the creation of the world to be holy and blameless in His sight. In love He predestined us to be adopted as His sons through Jesus Christ" (Ephesians 1:4,5). There was never a moment when God did not purpose in His love to make the ultimate sacrifice for us. He planned to leave heaven's glory, beauty, and peace and take on the body of a man. You and I, who are not even worthy to call His name, are so loved that we have always been on His mind! This is such an essential concept to teach to children. Many are searching for something or someone who will love them this much.

The greatest love our heavenly Father expressed to us was sending His Son, Jesus Christ, to be our Savior. When we receive Jesus as our Savior and Lord, God envelops and infuses us with His everlasting love. We enter into a special eternal relationship with Him. John recognized this and exclaimed: "How great is the love the Father has lavished on us, that we should be called children of God!" (1 John 3:1). This love will be with us for eternity.

As you teach this lesson, emphasize that God loves us as no one on earth could ever love us. Explain that Jesus' death is the evidence of God's love. Show your students how much God loves them by sharing examples of His unconditional love in your life or in the life of others. Model this kind of love in your classroom. Also explain that God's love means that He extends to us His mercy. He is faithful and unchanging, so we can always depend on His love.

You may want to give students an opportunity to receive Jesus as their Savior during the Bible Story. If so, enlist the help of another adult to counsel these students in a separate area of your room. Provide children's gospel tracts such as *Would You Like to Belong to God's Family?* (See the Resources for ordering information.)

If you are using this book as a stand-alone curriculum rather than as a four-book discipleship series, you may choose to present *The Story of Jesus for Children* video as an additional lesson. This will allow you to present the life, death, and resurrection of Jesus within these three units and give a more complete picture of the Trinity. The video lesson is in the appendix. If you wish to keep within the thirteen-lesson time frame, add the video lesson right after this lesson and disregard the review, Lesson 13.

LESSON PLAN

OPENING ACTIVITY: God's Love Bears All

Have students share their Top Ten Lists. Compliment them for obeying God.

Set out the cups, books, slips of paper, tape, and pencils on a table in front of the students. Then ask:

- Who is one person whom you love a lot? (*My mom; my dad; my grandparent; my best friend.*)

- Why do you love this person? (*He loves me. She takes care of me. We spend a lot of time together.*)

Let's look at how strong our love is for the people we love—like our friends. We'll let these two cups represent our love for other people. **Ask a student to write "LOVE" on each of the cups.** How strong is your love? What can make your love for others weaker? Let's name some things that make people dislike someone.

Ask students to name one reason that it is difficult to love someone. Some examples may be: if that person doesn't act "cool"; if someone doesn't come from the right kind of family; when my friend and I fight. As each reason is given, write it on a slip of paper and tape it to one of the books until all ten books are labeled. Place the cups about six inches apart. One at a time, have students select one book, read the paper slip, and set the book on top of the cups. After two or three books are placed, the cups will collapse.

People's love for others can be very fragile. When people don't look or act right, many times our love for them doesn't hold up. But God's love will always hold up. No matter what we do, how we look, or where we come from, God will always love us.

Hold up the two bricks. Let's say that these bricks represent God's love for us. **Set bricks about six inches apart.** Now let's say these books represent things we do that displease God. **Remove the taped slips of paper from the books. Have students call out things we do that displease God, such as telling lies, stealing, swearing, or showing disrespect to parents. Write each suggestion on a new slip of paper. Ask volunteers to tape slips onto books and set them on top of the bricks.**

Look how strong God's love is. It continues to hold up under anything we can say or do. In fact, the Bible tells us that nothing can separate us from God's love.

Read Romans 8:38,39. Help your students name all the things mentioned in the verses. They are: death, life, angels, demons, present, future, height, depth, or anything in all of creation.

Actually, we can't measure God's love because it is so huge. It fills the universe and spills over. God describes Himself as our heavenly Father. In our Bible story, we'll see what a loving heavenly Father our God is.

BIBLE STORY: Eternal Love

> *Before Class:* Stuff the paper lunch bags with old newspapers and tape them closed to make "altar stones." Make one per student.

To begin activity, have kids sit in a circle. Ask:

- Has anyone ever asked you to do something so difficult that you were afraid to do it? Tell us about it. *(Allow volunteers to relate events.)*

- What is the most difficult test you have ever taken? This could be a physical test like a race, a test in school, or a test of a talent you have. *(Allow students to respond.)*

Today, we're going to learn about an unusual test. The Bible tells us about a time when God tested someone. Let's read the story. **Read Genesis 22:1–9, adding a lot of emphasis in story fashion. Stop after the first sentence in verse 9 where Abraham builds the altar.**

Let's build an altar like the one Abraham made. **Bring out the lunch-bag stones and build an altar by putting stones together with masking tape.** Now, let's read the rest of the story to see what happens. **Read Genesis 22:9–19, starting where you left off.**

- Why do you think God asked Abraham to sacrifice his son? *(To see if Abraham would obey. To show Abraham how God would provide.)*

This story of Abraham shows us something about God. What Abraham did is a picture of how much God loves us. Let's go through the story again to see what God is showing us about His love.

Write these points on the chalkboard as you give them. Read the verses that accompany each point.

1. Abraham had one son, Isaac, whom he loved very much.

   God had only one Son, Jesus, whom He loved very much (John 3:16).

2. Abraham was willing to give up his son to die when God told him to do it.

   God was willing to give up His Son to die for us (Romans 8:32).

3. God provided a ram to use as a sacrifice in place of Isaac.

   God provided His Son, Jesus, as the Lamb of God to take our place as sinners who deserve to die (John 1:29).

4. Abraham became the father of a great nation, Israel, through his son, Isaac, because he obeyed God.

   Jesus made the way for millions of believers to become part of God's family because He obeyed His heavenly Father and died for us (John 1:12).

   In the Old Testament, Abraham obeyed God and was willing to sacrifice his son to worship God. But God provided a substitute, a ram, and Isaac lived.

In the New Testament, God was willing to sacrifice His Son, Jesus, to pay for our sins. We are the ones who deserve to die to pay the penalty for our own sins. Instead, God substituted Jesus in our place. Jesus died and His blood was spilled for us.

That's how much God loves us. He gave up the most precious thing He had—His Son—for you! That's how much Jesus loves you. He was willing to come to earth, be born as a baby, grow up, and die on a cross for you!

Read Romans 8:38,39 again. Are you beginning to see how deep God's love is for you? Do you understand that He loves you right now, just as you are?

You don't have to be prettier or smarter or act better to have God love you more. You don't have to have money, live in the right place, go to the right church, or be born into a certain kind of family to have God love you. God loves you 100 percent, completely. He wants you to be part of His family—forever!

If you are planning to present a gospel tract to your students, do this now.

No one loves you as completely as God does. No one cares about you more than God does.

- How does it make you feel to know that God loves you so much? (*It makes me feel great! It makes me feel happy.*)

God showed us how much He loves us by one most special way, by sending Jesus, God's only Son, to become our Savior. That means that Jesus saved us from eternal punishment. Because of Jesus, we can become children of God and live with God in heaven forever. We can call God our Father. **Read 1 John 3:1.** Explain that the character traits your students have already learned, such as God's power, unlimited knowledge, and fairness, make Him the greatest Father we can have.

Have you thanked God and told Him how much you appreciate His love? Let's write down some special qualities of God's deep love.

Ask students to suggest words that describe God's love as you write them on the board. Guide the discussion to include these qualities: merciful, faithful, unchanging, and eternal.

Pull the stones off the altar and give one to each student. Make sure each student has a marker. Although no one of these qualities of God's love is more important than another one, at times in our lives, one quality can be more special to us than another. For example, when a person realizes he has done something very wrong, he will be thankful for God's mercy. If someone is feeling bad about herself, she will be glad that God's love is unchanging toward her.

- Which one of the qualities that we wrote on the board means the most to you right now? (*Go around the circle, having each person pick out one quality and tell why it is so important to them right now.*)

Write that quality on your altar stone. Then we will worship God with our stones.

Give students time to write, then lead them in solemnly placing their stones in a pile as they thank or praise God for that quality.

Optional Activity: Sing the chorus *For God So Loved the World.*

Emphasize the underlined words as you give these sentences. Because our heavenly Father loves us, He shows us mercy by forgiving our sins. He sent His Son to be our Savior. God is faithful to do everything He promises. And because God never changes, we can be sure that He will always love us!

- What five new character traits of God did I just mention? *(Loving, merciful, Savior, faithful, unchanging.)*

Let's put these qualities on our "God Is" diagram.

CHECK FOR UNDERSTANDING: God Is

Pass out pencils, and return each student's "God Is" diagram. If you have new students, have "God Is" handouts available to give them.

Now let's look at what we have learned about God's role as our Savior that we can add to our diagram.

Inside the darkest triangle, have students write "Savior" on the blank line on the left.

- How does God show us He loves us? *(He sent His Son to die for us. He gives us what we need every day.)*

Under "Savior" in the lighter triangle, have students write "loving." On the three blank lines at the edge of the triangle, have students write "merciful," "faithful," and "unchanging."

- Which quality that we just wrote on our diagram impresses you most about God? *(Allow for individual responses.)*

- How do those qualities of God the Father make you feel? *(Allow for individual responses.)*

God cares about us more than our parents do. He sees everything we do, hears everything we say, and knows everything we think. Yet He still loves us. No one can care for us like God does.

Now our diagram is complete. Look at all the awesome qualities of God. Aren't you glad that we serve a God like this? **Students can take diagrams home with them.**

LESSON ACTIVITY: Caring Tour

> *Before Class:* Write each of these words on separate pieces of paper to use as signs: Compassion; Mercy; Faithfulness. Set up three activity centers. They could be as simple as a chair with one of the signs taped on the wall behind the chair.
>
> Make one copy of the "Caring Tour" handout and the patterns on the "Suitcase Stuffings" page. Cut out the items on both photocopies. If you have an old badge, tape the "I forgive you" badge pattern over it. In a small suitcase, place the "Free Hug," "Free Friendship," "Free Laugh," and "Free Time" tickets. Also include several facial tissues, the "I forgive you" badge, praying hands (you could substitute a plastic replica if you have one available), artificial flower bouquet, and a Bible.

Select three good readers/actors to play the parts of "Weeping Willy/Wendy," "Fickle Fran/Fred," and "Sick Sadie/Sam," and give each actor the appropriate script. Send one actor to each center: "Weeping Willy/Wendy" goes to the Compassion center, "Fickle Fran/Fred" to the Mercy center, and "Sick Sadie/Sam" to the Faithfulness center. Instruct actors to read their scripts when the class arrives at their center.

Gather remaining students around you. Show them what you have in the suitcase. God wants His children to do something special to show their gratitude for His Son's sacrifice. God wants us to pass His love on to others. We are going on a Caring Tour. We will use what we have in this suitcase to help the people we meet. This way, we'll be able to act out ways we can be an example of love to others like our heavenly Father shows love to us.

Go to the Compassion center first. Have the actor read the script. Then ask students to give this person "Free Hug" tickets and tissues from the suitcase. Encourage students to pretend to soothe the actor.

Have the first actor join the Tour group. Go to the Mercy center. Have "Fickle Fran/Fred" read the script. Ask someone to tape the "I forgive you" badge on this actor. Have students express forgiveness and offer the actor the "Free Friendship" tickets.

Have the second actor join the Tour group. Go on to the Faithfulness center. Have "Sick Sadie/Sam" read the script. Ask one student to give Sadie/Sam the flowers, and other students to read the "Free Laugh" tickets and give them to the actor.

Have all students sit in a circle.

- When we heard the story of Willy/Wendy, whose parents are divorcing, how did we act like our heavenly Father toward that person? *(We were sad with him/her; we showed that we cared about his/her problem.)*

- When we heard the story of Fran/Fred, how did we act like our heavenly Father? *(We forgave our friend. We stayed friends even though we might be hurt again.)*

- When we heard the story of Sadie/Sam, how did we act like our heavenly Father? *(We tried to cheer him/her up. We listened to his/her story.)*

We still have some items in our suitcase. **Show what's left—the praying hands, Bible, and "Free Time" tickets.** When we show others that we care about them, we can't forget to show our heavenly Father that we care about Him, too. As I hold up each item, you tell me how it can show our love to God.

Hold up "Free Time" tickets. *(Making sure we spend time with God.)*

Hold up praying hands. *(Talking to God.)*

Hold up Bible. *(Reading God's Word, listening to what He says to us.)*

God loves us so much that He cares about every detail of our lives. Because He loves us so much, we should show Him how much we love Him too. Spending time with Him is a good way to do that. **Collect all tickets to use in the last activity of this lesson.**

MEMORY VERSE ACTIVITY: No Barriers

Romans 8:38,39—"I am convinced that neither death nor life, neither angels nor demons, neither the present nor the future, nor any powers, neither height nor depth, nor anything else in all creation, will be able to separate us from the love of God that is in Christ Jesus our Lord."

 Teaching Tip: If cardboard bricks are not available from a preschool classroom, use additional paper-bag stones.

Write the verse on the chalkboard. Using the bricks, set up a wall in the center of the room. Gather on one side of the wall. Talk about how a wall is a barrier to keep people out. Then explain that there are no barriers between God's love and us.

Lead your group in saying the verse several times. Now that we are familiar with the verse, let's act out what it says. Let's take down the barrier of bricks. I'll choose one person to come and take a brick from the top of the wall. When you take a brick, name one thing in the verse that cannot keep us from God's love. **Choose students one at a time to take a brick off the wall and name a barrier. After each block is removed, have the class recite the verse. Do this until the entire wall has been removed. Then say as a group,** "Absolutely nothing can separate us from the love of God."

APPLICATION: Mercy! Mercy!

God expects us to extend mercy to others just as He extended mercy to us. As I read the following situations, think about what your first reaction might be. Then tell me how God would want you to react. **Read each situation, giving students time to think. Then discuss what a good reaction might be. Suggestions are given in parentheses.**

SITUATION ONE

Jim is the most popular guy in your class. He wears all the right clothes and everyone considers him "cool." But every time you see him, you remember the day he embarrassed you in front of the whole class. Your teacher paired you with him for a science project. Most of the project was his idea, but when the project flopped during your class presentation, he blamed the whole idea on you. People in class still tease you about your failure. No one will believe that Jim was really responsible.

Today in class, the teacher pairs you with Jim again. She gives each pair ten minutes to solve a logic problem. Jim tells you that he can do this by himself without your help. You have the right answer. You see a panicked expression on Jim's face, and you know he can't get the answer. He is going to look like a fool in front of the class while you will look great. What should you do? (*Show mercy by helping your partner. Do not act proud.*)

SITUATION TWO

Kim is your best friend. Kim's sister was badly injured in a hit-and-run accident. She will spend the rest of her life in a wheelchair. She will never be the same again.

Kim's family was shocked to find out that the driver was a policeman who was drunk. Now he is charged with manslaughter and faces time in jail. His name is all over the newspapers.

Wherever you go, you hear people saying terrible things about the former policeman. Although you feel good about hearing people saying terrible things about this man, you know your feelings aren't right. And some of the things people are saying are untrue. What will you do? (*Ask God to help you feel mercy for the policeman even though he did something very bad. When people say untrue things about him, tell them what is true.*)

SITUATION THREE

You have an elderly neighbor who has a hard time walking. She doesn't like kids. Whenever you play basketball in your yard and your ball accidentally goes into her yard, she won't return the ball for several days. She yells at you for walking on her grass. All the kids in the neighborhood keep away from this lady's house.

One day you come home from school and discover dogs tearing up your neighbor's garbage can. Garbage is scattered all over her yard. You feel like she's getting what she deserves. But what should you do? (*Ask God to help you love your neighbor. Pick up the garbage for her.*)

WEEKLY ASSIGNMENT: Now On to Real Life

Distribute the "Suitcase Stuffings" handout and scissors to each student. Have students cut apart their tickets. Say, This week, use your tickets to help you remember to show love to God and to others.

Close in prayer, thanking God for being our heavenly Father and for sending His Son, Jesus. Ask Him to help your students show His love to others this week.

If you are planning to use *The Story of Jesus for Children* Video Lesson between Units 1 and 2, announce it now. You may even decide to show a clip of the video at this time to capture your students' attention.

Caring Tour

Compassion Center
Weeping Willy/Wendy

I'm so sad. I feel like my whole life is falling apart. I came home from school today and found out that my parents are splitting up. I know they've been fighting a lot, but I didn't think this would happen. Dad already had his things packed. He went out the door without even saying goodbye to me. I was standing right beside the door. He didn't even look at me. He just seemed so mad.

My Mom's been crying all day. I can't talk to her. Every time I try to ask her about Dad, she just cries louder. She turns her back on me.

I spent the rest of the day in my room. No one made dinner. My little brother stayed in his room. I don't know what's going to happen to all of us.

Mercy Center
Fickle Fran/Fred

I guess you heard all the bad things I said about you last week. I don't know what came over me. It's just that I was in the middle of the most popular crowd in school. They were all listening to what I was saying. I started talking, and it seemed like I couldn't quit.

I started saying things about you that weren't true. They all wanted to know how you got that good grade in math. I told the kids that you cheated on last week's math test. I said that's why you got the highest grade in class. I told them that because I usually get the highest grade and I wanted them to think that I'm the smartest person in class. They all believed what I said about you.

I'm really sorry I said all those things. I know you studied really hard. But I wanted to make my "B" look good. Later, I tried to tell the kids that you deserved the grade that you got on the test. But they just laughed.

Will you forgive me for saying those things behind your back?

Faithfulness Center
Sick Sadie/Sam

Hello. I haven't seen you in a while. It's such a beautiful day today. I've been cooped up in the house for weeks because I've been very sick. That's why I haven't had time to make your favorite cookies like I used to do every Thursday.

I'm on my way to the doctor's office in a few minutes. It just seems like I can't get well. I can't do the things I used to do. I can't take walks around the block with my dog. I can't get out and weed my flowerbeds anymore. I can't get out and enjoy the sunshine or cook myself a good meal. Getting old is very hard.

Suitcase Stuffings

Free Hug Ticket
This ticket entitles you to one free hug whenever you present it.

Free Friendship Ticket
This ticket entitles you to one hour of my time for helping with homework or chores.
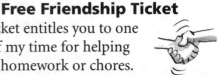

Free Hug Ticket
This ticket entitles you to one free hug whenever you present it.

Free Friendship Ticket
This ticket entitles you to one hour of my time for talking about anything.

Free Hug Ticket
This ticket entitles you to one free hug whenever you present it.

Free Friendship Ticket
This ticket entitles you to one hour of my time for playing games.

Time Ticket
Heavenly Father, I love You. I will spend ten minutes today talking to You in prayer.

Free Laugh Ticket
Why does a giraffe need such a long neck? *(Because its head is so far away from its body.)*

Time Ticket
Heavenly Father, I love You. I will spend ten minutes today reading Your Word, the Bible.

Free Laugh Ticket
What is the best way to catch a rabbit? *(Hide behind a bush and make a noise like a carrot.)*

Time Ticket
Heavenly Father, I love You. I will tell one person today how much You love him or her.

Free Laugh Ticket
What has four legs and goes, "Oom, oom"?
(A cow walking backwards.)

Who Is the Holy Spirit?

BOOK OBJECTIVE	To introduce students to God and help them understand His nature.
UNIT OBJECTIVE	To help students begin walking daily with the Holy Spirit.
LESSON 5: Getting to Know the Holy Spirit	*Objective:* To help students discover who the Holy Spirit is and why He came to earth. *Application:* To encourage students to ask the Holy Spirit to help them in everyday situations they face.
LESSON 6: Discovering What the Holy Spirit Does	*Objective:* To help students learn how the Holy Spirit helps them as believers. *Application:* To show students how they can turn their problems over to the Holy Spirit.
LESSON 7: Being Filled with the Holy Spirit	*Objective:* To help students learn how to be filled with the Spirit. *Application:* To encourage students to ask the Holy Spirit to produce the fruit of the Spirit in their lives.
LESSON 8: Walking in the Spirit	*Objective:* To help students learn how to practice walking in the Spirit daily. *Application:* To encourage students to begin practicing Spiritual Breathing.

Picture this scene. Jesus Christ is standing with His disciples on the Mount of Olives only moments before He is to ascend into heaven. He has commanded them to wait in Jerusalem for the coming of the Holy Spirit, whom the Father had promised.

The disciples are confused. They expect Jesus to set up an earthly kingdom, but He had greater plans for them. "When the Holy Spirit has come upon you," He explains, "you will receive power to testify about Me with great effect, to the people in Jerusalem, throughout Judea, in Samaria, and to the ends of the earth, about My death and resurrection" (Acts 1:8, TLB).

By these words, Jesus is suggesting that, although they had been with Him for more than three years, it was not enough that they had heard Him teach the multitudes and seen Him heal the sick and even raise the dead. He was emphasizing that they needed to be empowered with the Holy Spirit to be effective and fruitful as His witnesses throughout the world.

Later, the disciples were filled with the Holy Spirit, whose divine, supernatural power changed them from fearful men to radiant witnesses for Christ. They were used by God to help change the course of history. This same omnipotent power of the Holy Spirit is available to you and me to enable us to live holy and fruitful lives for Jesus Christ.

This power is also available to preteens. With all that our children face in our society, they need to have the enabling of the Holy Spirit to live holy lives.

This unit will introduce your students to the nature and mission of the Holy Spirit and give them practical steps for living as Spirit-filled believers. Your students will begin by learning about the day Jesus promised to send the Holy Spirit. They will then discover the supernatural results of asking God to fill them with the Holy Spirit. Finally, your student will apply the filling of the Spirit to their ongoing Christian adventure.

As you teach these lessons, apply the truths of the Holy Spirit and His mission to your life. Become an example of Spirit-filled living to those you teach. And experience the joyful results in your own daily experiences.

Getting to Know the Holy Spirit

LESSON PLAN

OBJECTIVE: Students will discover who the Holy Spirit is and why He came to earth.

APPLICATION: Students will learn how to ask the Holy Spirit to help them in everyday situations they face.

LESSON PLAN ELEMENT	ACTIVITY	TIME	SUPPLIES
Opening Activity	*Who Am I?*	7–10	"Up Close and Personal" handouts; pencils
Bible Story—John 16:5–16, Jesus promises to send the Holy Spirit	*Wind and Fire*	10–15	Bible; 2 pieces of paper; 2 pencils
Lesson Activity	*Character Cards*	9–10	10 pieces of white paper; markers; crayons; pencils; tape; Bibles
Memory Verse Activity	*Who? What?*	5–10	Dry-erase marker or chalk
Check for Understanding	*Spirit Survey*	3–5	"Up Close and Personal" handouts; pencils
Application	*What's in a Name?*	3–5	Paper; pencils
Weekly Assignment	*By the Book*	3–5	

D r. Edwin J. Orr, who was an authority on revival, described the Holy Spirit as "the Commander-in-Chief of the Army of Christ. He is Lord of the harvest, supreme in revival, evangelism, and missionary endeavor. Without His consent, plans are bound to fail. It behooves us as Christians to fit our tactical operations into the plan of His strategy, which is the reviving of the church and the evangelism of the world."

These sound like lofty words to apply to elementary-age children. Yet their Christian life is just as dependent on the Holy Spirit's power as the life of any believer. Their effectiveness as growing children of God is directly related to their experience as Spirit-filled followers of Christ.

Our children need to know that the Holy Spirit is not some vague, ethereal shadow or an impersonal force. He is equal in every way with the Father and with the Son. All divine attributes are ascribed to the Holy Spirit. He has infinite intellect (1 Corinthians 2:11), will (1 Corinthians 12:11), and emotion (Romans 15:30).

The first reference to the Holy Spirit is made in Genesis 1:2. His influence is noted throughout the Old Testament, but it becomes even more pronounced in the life and ministry of our Lord Jesus. Finally, after our Savior ascended to be at the right hand of the Father, the place of power, He sent the Holy Spirit to be our "Counselor" or "Helper" (John 14:26; 15:26). The Greek word for counselor or helper is *paraclete,* meaning the "one called alongside" the Christian as a companion and friend; also the one who energizes, strengthens, and empowers the believer in Christ.

In this lesson, your students will learn who the Holy Spirit is and why He came to earth. The activities will provide a foundation for later lessons in which students will learn how to be filled with the Spirit and how to walk in the Spirit. As you teach the concepts, be aware of any wrong ideas your students have about the Holy Spirit. Gently lead them into the truth about this third Person of the Trinity.

LESSON PLAN

OPENING ACTIVITY: Who Am I?

Look around the room. There are many of us in class today. We all look different and we all act and think differently. We each have our own personality. Some of us like to be in places that are quiet; others like exciting, noisy places. Some of us like to talk a lot; others like to listen. Some of us like games where we can compete to win; others like games where everyone wins. These things are all part of our personalities.

It's fun to get to know people with different personalities. Let's take a few minutes to interview someone to learn about that person. Just fill out the "Personality Survey" part of your worksheet.

Distribute the "Up Close and Personal" handouts and pencils. Have students form pairs and interview each other by filling out the "Personality Survey." When everyone is finished, go over some of the questions, allowing students to tell about their partners.

It's interesting to learn new things about each other's personalities. Today we're going to find out about the third Person of the Trinity—the Holy Spirit. He has a personality, and we can get to know Him too, just like we got to know more about God the Father and God the Son. Listen to a story about who the Holy Spirit is and how He came to live with us.

BIBLE STORY: Wind and Fire
Make sure students have Bibles.

- What comes to your mind when someone mentions the name Holy Spirit? (*Allow students to answer. Tailor your lesson to the misconceptions your students have about the Holy Spirit.*)

The Holy Spirit is a Person. As we learned in an earlier lesson, the Holy Spirit is one Person of the Trinity, along with God the Father and God the Son. He is not a ghost or a shadow or something that just floats along. He is a Person who is equal in every way with the other two members of the Trinity. All the personality traits that belong to God also belong to the Holy Spirit.

But each Person of the Trinity has a different role to play. God the Father sent Jesus the Son to die on the cross. God forgives our sins because Jesus paid the penalty for our sins. But what part does the Holy Spirit play in our lives?

Jesus began telling His disciples about the Holy Spirit when He was about to leave this earth and return to heaven. What would happen to the disciples when Jesus was no longer there? How would they know what to do for Him? How could they keep from getting discouraged? They still had so many questions about God and what God wanted them to do.

At the same time, Jesus wanted to make sure that His disciples were taken care of when He was gone. How could He do this?

He promised the disciples that He would send Someone to help them. This Person is still here helping us today. If you haven't guessed who this Person is, He is the Holy Spirit.

Let's read about what Jesus said. **Read John 16:5–16, having a different student read each verse. Be sensitive to those students who are not good readers.**

Divide the class into two groups, and give each group paper and pencils. Assign John 16:5–11 to one group and John 16:12–16 to the second group. Have each group designate one person as a recorder and one person as a reporter.

In your group, read the verses you were assigned. Identify some facts about God the Father, God the Son (Jesus), and God the Holy Spirit that you find in your passage of Scripture. Decide what each Person of the Trinity is doing. Have your recorder write down these facts. When you're finished, your reporter will report to the rest of the class on what you found. The words "Counselor" and "Spirit of truth" are names for the Holy Spirit.

Give groups time to read and write. Circulate among them, showing them some answers if they are having trouble finding what to write. Some answers are:

GROUP 1—JOHN 16:5–11

God the Father:

> *(He sent Jesus to earth.)*
> *(The Father is waiting in heaven.)*

Jesus the Son:

> *(He is going to heaven to be with the Father.)*
> *(He is going to send a Counselor to help the disciples.)*

Holy Spirit:

> *(He will convict the world of guilt for sin.)*
> *(He will convict the world of coming judgment.)*

GROUP 2—JOHN 16:12–16

God the Father:

> *(He owns all and has given it all to the Son.)*

Jesus the Son:

> *(He will get the glory.)*
> *(Everything that belongs to the Father is His.)*

Holy Spirit:

> *(He will guide people to the truth.)*
> *(He will tell us what is going to happen in the future.)*
> *(He will bring glory to the Son.)*

Have class reconvene and ask reporters to give their reports.

- If you had been one of the disciples that day, how do you think you would have felt hearing what Jesus had to say? (*Sad because Jesus was going away. Confused because I wouldn't understand who the Counselor was.*)

- What do you think Jesus meant when He said, "In a little while you will see Me no more, and then after a little while you will see Me"? (*Jesus would die and be buried. Then He would be raised again and visit the disciples.*)

- Why do you think Jesus thought it was so important to send the Holy Spirit? (*So the disciples would have a helper. The Holy Spirit was going to do some of the things that Jesus wouldn't be there to do.*)

What Jesus promised all happened when the Holy Spirit came to live within believers. He came forty days after Jesus died and was resurrected. What is amazing about this is that when Jesus was on earth, He could only be in one place at one time. The Holy Spirit can be in all places at all times. Jesus could only teach by telling the disciples what to do. The Holy Spirit teaches believers what to do by living inside them every moment of every day.

Today, the Holy Spirit is here, living inside believers, helping them obey God, helping them understand the Bible, helping them not to sin. Just like God the Father and God the Son, God the Holy Spirit does amazing and wonderful things. And the great thing about Him is that we can know Him too.

LESSON ACTIVITY: Character Cards

Divide students into ten groups. A group can be as small as one student. (If you have fewer than ten students, form five groups and assign each group two references to make two character cards.) Distribute paper, markers, crayons, pencils, and tape to the groups. Make sure students have Bibles.

What kind of personality do you have? We talked about that in our opening activity. The different parts of your personality are called character traits.

- What character traits do you have? (*Allow for individual responses.*)

We learned a little bit about what the Holy Spirit is like in the Bible story. Now let's investigate further to find out about His character traits. I will assign your group a certain aspect of the Holy Spirit's personality. Look up the verses and make a character card that will illustrate the character trait of the Holy Spirit that your verse describes. Your illustration could be of something that symbolizes that character trait, or something a Christian can do with the Holy Spirit's help, like understanding the Bible better, or an example of a Bible story, like the story we heard today about the Holy Spirit coming to help us. If your assigned verse has an "a" behind it, just use the first half of the verse. If your verse has a "b" behind it, use the second half of the verse.

Assign one of the following verses and descriptions to each group. Have students look up the verse and then write the description on the paper and illustrate the character trait. Give groups about five minutes to work.

John 14:26—He is a teacher.

Galatians 5:16—He keeps us from sin.

John 16:8—He convicts us of sin. (Convict means to make us feel sorry about our sin.)

Galatians 5:22—He develops godly character traits in us.

Acts 1:8—He gives us power to witness.

John 16:13a—He guides us into truth.

John 16:13b—He tells us what will happen in the future.

John 16:14—He helps us know the things of Jesus.

1 Corinthians 2:11—He knows the thoughts of God.

John 14:17—He lives in us.

When groups finish, have them read their verse from the Bible, then show and explain their character cards. Ask each group to tape their card to a board or wall. When all groups finish, review by reading each card together.

- Which of the Holy Spirit's character traits is the most important to you right now? Why? *(His teaching because I need help with lots of things. Keeping me from sin so I won't do wrong things.)*

- Which character traits explain how He can help us today? *(He lives in me so He can help me with hard things. He knows the thoughts of God so He knows what's going to happen and how it will happen.)*

MEMORY VERSE ACTIVITY: Who? What?

John 16:13—"When He, the Spirit of truth, comes, He will guide you into all truth. He will not speak on His own; He will speak only what He hears, and He will tell you what is yet to come."

Write John 16:13 on the chalkboard or whiteboard in the following way:

Who?   When He, the Spirit of Truth,

What?   comes,

Who?   He

What?   will guide you into all truth.

Who?   He

What?   will not speak on His own;

Who?   He

What?   will speak only what He hears, and

Who?   He

What?   will tell you what is yet to come.

Divide the class into two groups. Read the verse aloud to your students. This verse tells us that the Holy Spirit is our guide and that He will reveal the future to us. We will practice this verse by asking "who" and "what" interview questions. One side will ask "who" and "what" and the other side will answer with a word or phrase from the verse.

Go through the verse several times. Then have groups switch speaking parts and go through the verse several more times. For further practice, have students go through the interview questions in pairs.

CHECK FOR UNDERSTANDING: Spirit Survey

In our opening activity, you filled out a survey about your partner's personality. This helped you understand more about that person. Listening to the lesson today, you probably learned some unique characteristics of the Holy Spirit. Let's take a few minutes to fill out a survey on the Holy Spirit. You can use the character cards on the board (wall) to help you.

Have students take out their "Up Close and Personal" handout. The bottom half contains the Spirit Survey. Have students pair up with their original partners. Give pairs time to fill out the Spirit Survey. Then go over their answers with them and review the jobs and character of the Holy Spirit. The following are the correct answers:

SPIRIT SURVEY

Name: _Holy Spirit_

Came to earth: _Day of Pentecost_

Lives where: _in believers_

Jobs:

John 14:26 _teaches believers_

John 16:13a _guides believers to the truth_

John 16:13b _tells us what is to come_

John 16:14 _brings glory to God_

Things He does for me:

Galatians 5:16 _helps me avoid sin_

Galatians 5:22 _helps me have the fruits of the Spirit_

Acts 1:8 _helps me tell others about Jesus_

John 14:17 _lives within me_

APPLICATION: What's in a Name?

Each of us has a name or nickname that we like to be called.

- By what name or nickname do you like to be called? *(Allow for individual responses.)*

Names and nicknames can often tell us a lot about people. Many years ago, people had last names that described something about them. The Bakers probably owned a store that sold baked goods. Mr. Johnson was the son of John. Today, nicknames tell us about people. What do these nicknames tell us?

- Junior?

- Buddy?

- Doc?

The Bible has many names for the Holy Spirit. Each name tells us something about Him. **Give each student a piece of paper. Have students fold the paper in half, then in half again to make a four-page book. Make sure students have pencils.**

I will read four Bible verses that give a name of the Holy Spirit. Write one name on each page of your booklet. **Read verses and titles.**

Romans 8:2—Spirit of Life

John 16:13—Spirit of Truth

Hebrews 10:29—Spirit of Grace

Ephesians 1:13—Promised Holy Spirit

Now, on each page, write how you think that truth about the Holy Spirit can help you this week. For example, "Spirit of Life" means that the Holy Spirit gives us life to live as God wants us to live. So you could write, "The Spirit of Life will help me live without giving in to temptation this week." Do this for each of the Holy Spirit's names. "Grace" means that God gives us good things that we don't deserve, like eternal life with Him or answers to prayer.

Give students time to write. Circulate to help them come up with ideas. Then have students share what they have written. Help students who have inadequate answers to refine them.

WEEKLY ASSIGNMENT: By the Book

In this lesson, we learned who the Holy Spirit is and why He came to earth. But learning these things doesn't help us unless we let the Holy Spirit live in us and make us more like Jesus.

Another name for the Holy Spirit is our Comforter. That means that He comes alongside us when we feel bad or when we are discouraged.

- Think of a time when you sensed that God was with you during a hard time. What happened? *(Allow for individual responses.)*

DISCOVERING OUR AWESOME GOD

- How can the Holy Spirit comfort you this week? *(Allow for individual responses.)*

Through your students' responses, help them understand that they can take any problem to the Lord in prayer.

This week, take your booklet home and look for ways that the Holy Spirit can help you. Then when you are in a situation where you need the Holy Spirit's help to come alongside you, write that situation in your booklet. For example, if you feel alone at night, you could remember that God promises He will never leave you. You will know that the Holy Spirit is with you at that moment. Write about that time in your booklet on the page "Promised Holy Spirit."

Do this for all the pages in the book. Bring it with you to our next lesson and we will share the situations with each other.

Close in prayer, thanking the Holy Spirit for being present with each believer all the time.

Up Close and Personal

Personality Survey

Name: _____

Birthdate: _____ Age: _____

Favorite things:

Color: _____ Book: _____ TV show: _____

Movie: _____ Sport: _____ Food: _____

5 words that describe you: _____

Some things that bug you: _____

Your one wish is: _____

Sport or hobby you enjoy: _____

Your best school subject is: _____

In your future, you see: _____

Spirit Survey

Name: _____

Came to earth: _____

Lives where: _____

Jobs:

     John 14:26 _____

     John 16:13a _____

     John 16:13b _____

     John 16:14 _____

Things He does for me:

     Galatians 5:16 _____

     Galatians 5:22 _____

     Acts 1:8 _____

     John 14:17 _____

Discovering What the Holy Spirit Does

LESSON PLAN

OBJECTIVE: Students will learn how the Holy Spirit helps them as believers.

APPLICATION: Student will begin turning their problems over to the Holy Spirit.

LESSON PLAN ELEMENT	ACTIVITY	TIME	SUPPLIES
Opening Activity	*Double the Dough*	5–10	Dough (see activity for recipe); bowl; plastic wrap; extra package of dry yeast; ½ cup warm water; 1 tablespoon sugar
Bible Story—Assorted Scriptures, Peter's change	*Before and After Pictures*	10–15	Bibles; paper; pencils; markers
Lesson Activity	*Acting Our Part*	9–10	1 copy of "Do Your Part Action Cards" handout; envelope; wax for seal (can be made by dropping wax from a candle); play money; make-believe contract; moving boxes or suitcases
Application	*What a Situation!*	7–10	
Weekly Assignment	*Sealed for God*	3–5	Pencils; paper; envelopes
Memory Verse Activity	*Spirit Shouts*	3–5	2 pieces of paper; pen; Bibles
Check for Understanding	*The Dough Doubles*	3–5	Dough from Opening Activity

Through the centuries, many of Christ's followers have been ordinary people. Nothing spectacular ever happened to them or through them before they put their faith in Christ. Then, as happened to Peter on the day of Pentecost, their lives were dramatically changed when they were filled with the Holy Spirit. No longer ordinary or average, they became men and women of God—bold in faith and instruments of God's power.

Today, that same Holy Spirit—with His life-changing power—is available to each of us. Yet, tragically, multitudes of Christians go through life without ever experiencing the abundant and fruitful life that Christ promised to all who trust Him.

The Holy Spirit came to bear witness of the Lord Jesus Christ and to glorify Him (John 16:13,14). As Jesus had come to exalt and reveal the Father, the Holy Spirit was sent to exalt and glorify the Son, Jesus Christ. It logically follows, then, that the more we allow the Holy Spirit to control our lives, the more we will love and serve the Lord Jesus, and the more we will be conscious of His loving and abiding presence.

When we are filled with the Holy Spirit, we are filled with Jesus Christ. Thus, when we are filled with the Lord Jesus Christ, a power much greater than our own is released within us and through us for service and victorious living.

To accomplish His work in us, the Holy Spirit performs several vital functions. Some of these happened the moment we became children of God. Others are ongoing as we grow in spiritual maturity. The Holy Spirit regenerates us, comes to dwell in us, seals us in Christ, guarantees our inheritance, baptizes us into the body of Christ, and fills and empowers us for service.

Your students need to be assured of the work the Holy Spirit does for us. They need to see Him as a vital part of the Trinity in giving us salvation and keeping us safe within God's family.

LESSON PLAN

OPENING ACTIVITY: Double the Dough

Before Class: Make the dough using the following recipe:

> 1 cup warm water (the temperature of a baby's warmed milk, not scalding)
>
> 1 package dry yeast (check your yeast's date for freshness)
>
> 1 teaspoon salt
>
> 1 tablespoon sugar
>
> 2½–3 cups flour

Mix water, yeast, salt, and sugar in a bowl until yeast is dissolved. Add flour gradually until dough is stiff. Knead on a floured surface for about 5 minutes. Put into clean, lightly greased bowl.

Have the students who brought to class their booklets about the Holy Spirit share the ways the Holy Spirit has helped them.

Set the dough lump in front of your class. Read Acts 1:8. In this verse, Jesus is speaking to His followers.

- What does Jesus say will happen when we receive the Holy Spirit? *(We will receive power.)*

Remember, we learned that the Holy Spirit is God. When we have God filling us, a power much greater than our own lives in us. The Holy Spirit's power helps us serve God better and helps us overcome sin.

Let's do a demonstration to understand how this works. **Gather around a table. Hold up the package of yeast.**

- Does anyone know what this is? *(Yeast.)*

- What is it used for? *(To make bread rise.)*

Open the package and let the students see the yeast. This doesn't look like much, but it is an important ingredient in making bread. Yeast helps the bread dough rise and become full and light.

Dissolve the yeast in warm water for a minute. Mix in 1 tablespoon of sugar. Have students watch until the mixture bubbles. The bubbles show a little of the yeast's power.

Show the students the bowl of dough you made earlier. This dough is made with yeast. We are going to watch it over the next hour and see what happens. We can let the bread dough with yeast represent the life of a person who has the Holy Spirit living in him. When we ask Jesus to be our Savior, the Holy Spirit comes into our lives, even though we don't look any different on the outside.

- What do you think will happen in the dough with yeast? *(It will get bigger. It will be more like bread dough.)*

- How is having the Holy Spirit in our lives like having yeast in dough? *(We won't stay the same. Our lives will get bigger and better.)*

- What difference do you think having the Holy Spirit in our lives will make for us? *(He will help us. He makes things happen in our lives.)*

In our lesson today, we'll find out what the Holy Spirit does in our lives and what difference that makes to us. Right now, I'm going to set this dough in a warm place. We will come back later to see what has happened to it. **Set the dough in a warm place and cover it with plastic wrap.**

BIBLE STORY: Before and After Pictures

Before Class: Write each set of phrases and verses on a separate piece of paper as shown below:

BEFORE PICTURE

A. Slow to understand—Matthew 15:15–17

B. Rebuked Jesus about His death—Matthew 16:21,22

C. Cowardly—Matthew 26:56–58

D. Not much power to heal—Mark 9:17,18

E. Denied Jesus—Mark 14:67–71

AFTER PICTURE

A. Brave—Acts 4:13

B. Taught about Jesus' death and resurrection—1 Peter 1:18–21

C. Preached with boldness—Acts 4:8–10

D. Did many miracles—Acts 5:15,16; 9:40

E. Proclaimed Jesus when arrested—Acts 5:29–33

Just as dough cannot rise and change into something good on its own, we cannot change into a person who obeys God and does good without the presence of the Holy Spirit. If we don't let the Holy Spirit work in our lives, we will not change for the good.

But when we let the Holy Spirit change us, we are able to do things we could never do before. Our attitudes change. Our actions change. Even our outlook on life changes.

The Bible gives us the story of one man who was totally changed by the power of the Holy Spirit. He was filled with the Holy Spirit after Jesus went to heaven. This person was Peter, one of the twelve disciples.

Have you ever seen "before" and "after" weight-loss pictures in magazines? The "before" picture shows someone who is overweight and the "after" picture shows the same person who has lost a lot of weight after dieting.

Today, we'll make "before" and "after" pictures of Peter. Let's see how much he changed through the power of the Holy Spirit.

Divide the class into two groups. Give each group a piece of paper, pencils, and markers. Have each group assign one person to be the recorder who will write down the group's suggestions; one person to be an artist who will draw a picture after the group discussion; and five reporters who will tell about the characteristic for each letter. For example, one person in the "before" group will take "A" and tell how Peter had a hard time understanding spiritual truth. Another person will take "B," and so on. Groups will read each passage and discuss how it illustrates the characteristic. The recorder will write down what the group decides is important to report to the class.

Once all the passages have been read and discussed, each group will draw a picture of Peter as he was described in the passages. For example, the "before" group could draw a scared look on Peter's face and the "after" group an excited look.

Give students time to read, discuss, write, and draw. Then have groups share what they learned by describing the "before" and "after" characteristics one at a time. (The "before" group will report their findings on point "A," then the "after" group will report their findings on point "A," and so forth.) When you finish all characteristics (from A to E), have groups share their drawings.

- What differences did you see in Peter from the two drawings? *(Allow for individual responses.)*

- What was Peter like in the "before" picture? *(Scared; didn't have any power; crumbled under pressure.)*

- What was Peter like in the "after" picture? *(Brave; smart about spiritual things; could do lots of miracles.)*

The difference between Peter before and after Jesus' death and resurrection was that before he was living in his own power and after he was filled with the Holy Spirit. Here is the interesting fact about Peter's change. Peter spent three years with Jesus, learning from Jesus, watching Him do miracles. Yet, that did not change Peter into a strong, brave believer. It was only when the Holy Spirit came into Peter's life that he began to change. Then he had the power to obey the things he learned from Jesus. After that, Peter could stand up for what he believed.

God doesn't want us to merely change our outward behavior. That really doesn't work because when things get tough, our outward behavior turns ugly. God wants to change us from the inside. Then our outward behavior will reflect what we are inside. Then when things get tough, we can stand up to the pressure.

The Holy Spirit living in us is what changes us from the inside. The Holy Spirit does many things for us. Our Lesson Activity will show us several of these.

LESSON ACTIVITY: Acting Our Part

Before Class: Cut the "Do Your Part Action Cards" handout into five sections. Set out the props (envelope, wax for seal, play money, make-believe contract, moving boxes or suitcases).

A Christian is someone who has trusted Jesus Christ as Savior. The moment you became a Christian, the Holy Spirit came into your life. He did some special things for you. Let's find out what these things are.

Divide your class into five groups. Assign a narrator in each group; the remaining group members will be actors.

Give each group one action card, and instruct them to use the props as needed. Have groups follow the instructions on their cards. Give groups a few minutes to practice, then have them act out their actions. When they're all finished, gather for a discussion time.

- Why is it so important that the Holy Spirit first change our inward nature rather than starting with our outward behavior? *(Our inward behavior determines our outward behavior. Our inward nature is what makes us act like we do.)*

- What do our actions show about what's inside our hearts? *(What we do when we're in trouble shows what we are like inside. The Holy Spirit changes our hearts so we can do good things.)*

If you dropped a cone with your favorite flavor of ice cream in the dirt, would you want someone to pick it up, try to clean it off, and give it back to you? No, that wouldn't be good at all. Instead, you'd want someone to give you a new cone.

That's how the Holy Spirit works in our lives. He doesn't try to clean up our old, sinful nature. He comes in and seals us so that we will always be God's children. He also gives us a new nature that wants to obey God. Then He gives us the power to change the bad behavior and attitudes we are still holding on to from our old nature and habits. The Holy Spirit does the work; we only need to allow Him to have complete control of our lives.

APPLICATION: What a Situation!

Gather in a circle. I'm going to read some situations. After I finish, I want you to tell me what part of this person's life he or she has not given over to the Holy Spirit's control. Then I will ask, "What do you think will happen because the Holy Spirit is not in control?"

Then we will think about the situation to see what might happen if the person gives the situation over to the Holy Spirit's control.

Read each situation. After each, ask, "What do you think will happen because the Holy Spirit is not in control?" **After a discussion, read the situation again and discuss how that person could benefit from turning the problem over to God. Suggestions for asking for the Holy Spirit's help are in parentheses.**

SITUATION 1:

Kenji comes from a large family of seven children. His family is vacationing in Yellowstone National Park. The family parks their RV in a camping site. His parents start preparing dinner. They tell the kids that they can explore, but not to go too far away.

Kenji loves the forest. He loves smelling the pine trees and walking in their shadows. He's not worried about getting lost. He has a good sense of direction. He knows no one will miss him for a while because there are so many people in his family.

Kenji starts investigating many things in the forest. After a while, the sun starts to go down. Things don't look the same in the dusky light. Which way should he take to go back?...

(At that moment, Kenji should confess his disobedience. Then he can ask God to help him find the way back. In the future, he should ask the Holy Spirit to help him listen to and obey his parents' rules.)

SITUATION 2:

Jasmine has a difficult time in math. She studies, but finds it hard to pass the tests. Her best friend, Tanya, is really good in math. She has even won some awards in math.

Jasmine and Tanya sit close to each other in school. On the next test she takes, Jasmine can't understand the first problem. She doesn't know what to do. She looks up at Tanya's paper...

(Right then, Jasmine needs to ask the Holy Spirit to help her keep her eyes on her own paper. Later, she can ask the Holy Spirit to help her understand math and to help her find someone who can help her study. Then she can pray before each test.)

SITUATION 3:

Todd has a younger brother, Tim, who always bothers him. Whenever Todd's friends come over, Tim listens in on their conversations. Tim always wants to play with Todd's things.

One day, Tim invites a friend to stay the night. Tim and his friend want to play with Todd's video games. Immediately, Todd says, "No way!"...

(Right then, Todd can ask the Holy Spirit to give him wisdom on what to say to Tim. Perhaps Todd can supervise while Tim and his friend play. Todd can even help Tim and his friend learn some of the secret codes in the game. Later, Todd can ask the Holy Spirit to give him more love and patience for his brother—even when he's a pest.)

WEEKLY ASSIGNMENT: Sealed for God

Give each student an envelope, pencil, and piece of paper. Ask students to write down one situation they need to turn over to the Holy Spirit's control. Give them a few minutes to write.

Now we will pray, turning our situations over to the Holy Spirit's control. As I pray, you pray silently with me. When I pause, silently ask God to help you with the situation you wrote about on your paper.

Pray: Dear heavenly Father, I am so glad that you sent the Holy Spirit to help me live a godly life. I am also glad that the Holy Spirit is my guarantee that I will always be in your family. Right now I have a situation that I haven't been letting You control. I'm asking the Holy Spirit to help me do what's right in this situation. **Pause for a few seconds to allow students to pray silently.** Thank You, Father, that You answer my prayers. In Jesus' name, amen.

Now take the piece of paper on which you wrote your situation and put it into the envelope. Seal it to show that you have given your situation over to the Holy Spirit's control. **Allow a few moments for students to seal their envelopes. Have them write their names on their envelopes.**

This coming week, if you encounter the situation you wrote about, immediately ask the Holy Spirit to help you do what's right. You may have to pray one time or many times.

When we meet for our next lesson, we'll open our envelopes and discuss how the Holy Spirit helped us in our situations. **Either allow students to take envelopes home if you are sure they will bring them back, or collect them and make sure students remember to work on their situation during the week.**

MEMORY VERSE ACTIVITY: Spirit Shouts

Romans 12:1—"Therefore, I urge you, brothers, in view of God's mercy, to offer your bodies as living sacrifices, holy and pleasing to God—this is your spiritual act of worship."

Romans 12:2—"Do not conform any longer to the pattern of this world, but be transformed by the renewing of your mind. Then you will be able to test and approve what God's will is—his good, pleasing and perfect will."

Cut a piece of paper in half, and write one verse on each half. Roll each paper half into a scroll so the verses can be opened and read like an announcement.

Choose two students to be town criers. In days gone by, much of the important news was shouted out by a town crier. He also shouted out official announcements. In our Bible story, Peter was like a town crier when he preached the good news of Jesus Christ from the street corner.

Today, we are going to practice our verses in that way to remind us of how we should surrender control of our lives to the Holy Spirit.

Have one town crier read Romans 12:1 and the other read Romans 12:2. Repeat, choosing different students to take each part. After several times, pair students and have them practice the verse as town criers by using their Bibles.

CHECK FOR UNDERSTANDING: The Dough Doubles

Gather your students around the lump of dough. It should be much larger than before. Discuss how exciting it is when your dough rises as you're making bread. Then apply that to the excitement we will feel when the Holy Spirit works in our lives to make us more like Jesus.

Close in prayer, asking God to help your students give Him control over every area of their lives. Remind students of their Weekly Assignment.

Optional Activity: If you have time, form dough lump into 12 buns and bake at 350 degrees for 25 to 35 minutes. The buns are done when they are golden on top and sound hollow when tapped on top. Then serve the buns to your students.

Do Your Part Action Cards

....

The Holy Spirit Lives in Us

Narrator reads: The Holy Spirit dwells in us. First Corinthians 3:16 says, "Don't you know that you yourselves are God's temple and that God's Spirit lives in you?"

Act out a family welcoming someone new coming to live with them. Use boxes and/or suitcase.

Narrator reads: This is a picture of what happens in our life when we accept Jesus as Savior. The Holy Spirit comes into our life and lives with us.

....

The Holy Spirit Changes (Regenerates) Us

Narrator reads: The Holy Spirit changes us from the inside out. Titus 3:5 says, "He saved us through the washing of rebirth and renewal by the Holy Spirit."

Act out a person who is unhappy, mad, etc. Then have him or her pray to receive Jesus as Savior and become a joyful person.

Narrator reads: This shows us a picture of the change that occurs in us through the Holy Spirit when we receive Jesus as our Savior.

....

The Holy Spirit Seals Us

Narrator reads: The Holy Spirit seals our salvation so that we never have to be afraid that we are not part of God's family. Ephesians 4:30 says, "Do not grieve the Holy Spirit of God, with whom you were sealed for the day of redemption."

Act out someone writing a letter and sealing it.

Narrator reads: This shows that the Holy Spirit is our seal at the time of our salvation. No one can break the seal, so our salvation is safe.

The Holy Spirit Is Our Guarantee

Narrator reads: The Holy Spirit is our guarantee that we will one day receive our spiritual inheritance in heaven. Second Corinthians 5:5 says, "Now it is God who has made us for this very purpose and has given us the Spirit as a deposit, guaranteeing what is to come."

Act out someone giving play money as a down payment on a house or car and then signing a contract.

Narrator reads: When your mom and dad buy a house or car, they need to give a down payment and sign a contract as proof that they will pay the full amount of the loan. In a similar way, the Holy Spirit is our proof that one day we will receive an inheritance in heaven.

The Holy Spirit Empowers Us for Service

Narrator reads: The Holy Spirit empowers us so that we can serve others. Acts 1:8 says, "You will receive power when the Holy Spirit comes on you; and you will be my witnesses in Jerusalem, and in all Judea and Samaria, and to the ends of the earth."

Act out a king commissioning or empowering soldiers to act in his behalf.

Narrator reads: Just as these soldiers have the power or authority of the king, the Holy Spirit gives us power to serve others to help them become part of His kingdom.

LESSON 7

Being Filled with the Holy Spirit

LESSON PLAN

OBJECTIVE: Students will learn how to be filled with the Spirit.

APPLICATION: Students will ask the Holy Spirit to produce the fruit of the Spirit in their lives.

LESSON PLAN ELEMENT	ACTIVITY	TIME	SUPPLIES
Opening Activity	*What Am I Doing?*	5–10	
Bible Story—Acts 6 and 7, Stephen	*Pick a Cup*	10–15	27 small paper cups; marker; Bible
Lesson Activity	*In Which Circle Are You?*	9–10	Brown, yellow, green, and red construction paper; masking tape; Bible
Check for Understanding	*Life Circles*	3–5	"Life Circles" handouts
Application	*Rainbow Character*	7–10	Milk; 11"×13½" pan; milk; 4 food colorings; knife
Memory Verse Activity	*Fruit Basket Upset*	3–5	
Weekly Assignment	*Spiritual Fruit Basket*	3–5	"Spiritual Fruit Basket" handouts

T he Spirit-filled life is the Christ-filled life. The Spirit-filled Christian is one who, according to Romans 6:11, considers himself dead to sin but alive to God in Christ Jesus. The One who has been given "all authority in heaven and on earth" (Matthew 28:18) and in whom "all the fullness of the Deity lives in bodily form" (Colossians 2:9) can now express that power through the Spirit-filled believer. The One who came to seek and to save the lost now begins to seek the lost through the Christian. He directs the Christian's steps to those who are lost and in need. He begins to use the Christian's lips to tell of His love. His great heart of compassion becomes evident in the life of the Spirit-filled Christian.

In a very real sense, the Christian gives up his life, his spiritual impotence, defeat, and fruitlessness for the power and victory of Jesus Christ. This is what the great missionary statesman Hudson Taylor referred to as the "exchanged life."

When we are filled with the Holy Spirit, we are filled with Jesus Christ. We no longer think of Christ as One who helps us do some kind of Christian task but, rather, Jesus Christ does the work through us. He does not want us to work for Him. He wants us to let Him do His work in and through us.

Paul writes, "The life I live in the body, I live by faith in the Son of God, who loved me and gave Himself for me" (Galatians 2:20). When we yield our will to God the Holy Spirit and acknowledge that Jesus Christ is in fact in our life moment by moment, we will begin to draw on His life and power to do what God has intended for us.

Most young people think that they must work hard to please God. They think that they have to earn favor by doing good things in their own power. This erroneous thinking will lead to defeat and discouragement—no matter what age you are. In this lesson, emphasize that we serve God best when we step aside and let His Holy Spirit do the work in and through us. He gives us the power and the strength. We just bring our attitude of yieldedness to God.

Before you begin this lesson, make sure you understand how to be filled with the Holy Spirit and sincerely ask God to fill you with His Holy Spirit. You can learn how to be filled with the Spirit by studying this lesson or by ordering the booklet *Have You Made the Wonderful Discovery of the Spirit-Filled Life?* To order, see the Resources at the back of the book.

OPENING ACTIVITY: What Am I Doing?

To begin your lesson, have students open their sealed envelopes and explain how they let the Holy Spirit empower them to control the situation.

Have students form a circle. I am going to ask for a volunteer to be "It." The goal of the game is for "It" to guess what job, such as carpenter, doctor, or teacher, we are acting out. "It" will leave the room so that he or she cannot hear us. We will select a job and assign one person to lead us in our actions. We can do only what the leader does. Then I will ask "It" to come back into the room and stand in the middle of the circle. The leader will begin doing the action and we have to follow whatever our leader does. When "It" guesses the right job, I'll pick another student to be "It."

Play the game for a few rounds until everyone has had a chance to be the leader or "It." Then sit in a circle and discuss the following questions.

- When you were "It," what made it easy or hard to guess what the leader was doing? *(It was easy when the leader took his time to act out the job in the right way. It was hard because the job was a tough one to guess.)*

- Just like we watched the leader do his actions, in real life your friends watch you to see the kinds of things you are doing. What do they watch you do and when do they watch you? *(My friends watch me play soccer at recess. I'm good at math so my friends want to know how to do what I'm doing on my math sheets.)*

- People watch Christians to see what they do too. What kinds of things do people watch Christians do? *(Pray; help each other; go to church.)*

- Then why do you think it is so important for Christians to do the right thing? *(Because other people might not love God if they think Christians are not nice. We need to act like Christ did.)*

In our lesson today, we'll learn how to act like a child of God in our everyday life. You will be surprised at how simple it is to do what God wants us to do.

BIBLE STORY: Pick a Cup

Before Class: With a marker, write each of the fruits of the Spirit on a paper cup. They are: love, joy, peace, patience, kindness, goodness, faithfulness, gentleness, self-control. Make three sets of cups.

Many Christians think they are pretty good at acting like a child of God when things are going well for them. For example, we know that God wants us to tell others about Jesus. When we tell someone about Jesus and that person gets excited about what he or she hears, we are happy. But what happens when people make fun of us for believing in Jesus? Do we still tell more people about Jesus?

When we have the Holy Spirit in our lives, we will do what God wants us to do—no matter how hard it is to do it.

Stephen was one of the very first Christians. He loved Jesus with all of his heart. He was also what the Bible calls "filled with the Holy Spirit." **Read Ephesians 5:18.** That means that Stephen let the Holy Spirit control every part of his life. He was like a cup, filled to the brim with the Holy Spirit's love, joy, and peace.

Divide students into three groups. Give each group one set of cups. Have a small table or stand next to your chair.

I am going to read Stephen's story from the Bible. I will read a few verses, then stop. When I do, in your group decide which good characteristic you see in Stephen's life. Set the cup you choose on this table. Make sure your group can explain why you picked that characteristic.

Read Acts 6:8–15. Give groups a chance to discuss, select a cup, and set it on the table. Ask groups to explain their choice. There can be a variety of answers as long as the group has a good reason for choosing that quality. For example, one good choice is patience because Stephen did not reply immediately when his enemies accused him.

Then read Acts 7:51–53. One suggestion is faithfulness because Stephen was faithful to God.

Then read Acts 7:54–59. Explain that "fell asleep" means he died. One suggestion is love because he loved his enemies. Then discuss:

- How were Stephen's actions different from the way people normally act in similar circumstances? *(He didn't hate his enemies. He stood up for God even when it meant he would be killed.)*

- Why do you think people thought his face looked like an angel when he was filled with the Holy Spirit? *(He looked so peaceful. He was very kind and loving. He looked different from most people.)*

- How do you think being filled with the Holy Spirit would change the way you look? *(I would have a smile on my face more often. I would look kinder.)*

- What do you think being filled with the Holy Spirit is all about? *(Allow students to respond. Note their wrong ideas about being filled with the Spirit so you can address these thoughts during the discussion after the Lesson Activity.)*

In our Lesson Activity, we'll learn what it means to be filled with the Holy Spirit. This is the secret to living an exciting Christian life.

LESSON ACTIVITY: In Which Circle Are You?

 Before Class: You will be recreating the Life Circles from the "Life Circles" hand-out. Use them as patterns for this activity.

Cut 10 large circles from yellow construction paper. Cut two large "S's" from brown construction paper. Cut 10 large circles from green construction paper and two large crosses from red paper. Write one of the following phrases on each yellow circle: jealousy; worry; being discouraged; swearing; lying; cheating; gossiping; disobeying parents; not praying; not reading the Bible. Write one of the following phrases on each green circle: love; joy; peace; patience; kindness; faithfulness; goodness; prays; obeys God; tells others about Jesus.

Using masking tape, make two large circles (each about 5 feet in diameter) on the floor. Place a chair in the middle of each circle.

Gather students around the circles on the floor.

The Bible tells us how to be filled with the Holy Spirit. Earlier, we read Ephesians 5:18. This is what God commands us to do. **Read the verse again.** Anything that God commands us to do, He makes sure we are able to do it. Look at the promise in 1 John 5:14,15. **Read verses.**

To be filled with the Spirit, we need to make sure we don't have any sin in our lives, and then ask God to fill us with His Spirit. All we have to do is let God be in complete control of our lives—every single part, every single moment. Let's look at how this works.

Choose two students (student A and student B) to sit on the chairs in the circles. These circles represent a person's life. In the first circle, we have a person (student A) who doesn't let God control his life. Each of us has a throne or control center in our lives, represented by this chair. That control center shows who we let control our lives, who's the boss. This first circle will show what happens when we try to control our own lives.

Hand student A an "S." This "S" means that this person has "self" in control of his life. He does what he wants to do no matter who it hurts or how wrong it is. **Set a cross on the floor inside the circle.** This cross represents Jesus. Even though this person is a Christian and Christ is in his life, Christ is not in control. Jesus is not on the throne.

When we control our own life instead of letting the Holy Spirit control it, our life becomes a mess. **Hand the yellow circles to students. Have them put the circles inside the masking-tape circle in messy order one at a time, reading what is written on each circle as it is placed.** Look at what a mess this person is in!

Move to the second circle. Now, we'll say that this person has asked to be filled with the Holy Spirit. That means that he wants Jesus to control his life. **Hand a cross to student B.** Of course, "self" is still important (**put the second "S" on the floor inside the circle**), but "self" is not running this person's life.

Hand out the green circles to your students. When we let Jesus control our life and ask to be filled with the Holy Spirit, God makes our life wonderful, exciting, and fruitful. **Have students place the green circles in neat order inside the edge of the masking-tape circle, reading the phrases as the circles are placed. Then ask:**

- Why do you think there is so much difference between the self-controlled life and the life that is filled with the Holy Spirit? *(God makes the difference. The Holy Spirit makes our lives better.)*

- What do we have to do to be filled with God's Holy Spirit? *(Just ask to be filled and God will fill us.)*

- Does God ever break His promises? How do you know? *(God never breaks His promises because He never lies. We can always trust God to do what He says He will do because the Bible tells us this.)*

When we ask to be filled with the Holy Spirit, God will do just that. The only thing that will keep us from being filled with the Holy Spirit when we ask is if we have sin in our lives that we haven't confessed. We will be learning more about that in our next lesson. But right now, let's review what we've learned.

CHECK FOR UNDERSTANDING: Life Circles

Pass out the "Life Circles" handouts. Go over the two circles, discussing the differences between each life. Then ask:

- Which circle represents your life? *(Begin by explaining how you asked God to be filled with the Holy Spirit before the class time. Then allow volunteers to answer the question. Do not pressure anyone to answer.)*

Right now, we will take a minute to silently examine our own lives to see if we have any sin we have not confessed to God. Bow your head and talk to God. Talk to Him like a heavenly Father. Do not look at your neighbor as you pray. **Give students a few moments to do this.**

If you know that you don't have any unconfessed sin in your life, ask the Holy Spirit to fill you. We will be silent for a moment so we can pray. **Give students a few moments to do this.**

If you sincerely asked the Holy Spirit to fill you, He did. You may not feel any different, but He still filled you. Now let's look at what God will do with a person who is filled with the Holy Spirit.

APPLICATION: Rainbow Character

I'm going to give you a list of things called the fruits of the Holy Spirit: love, joy, peace, patience, kindness, goodness, faithfulness, gentleness, and self-control. **Read Galatians 5:22,23.** We have already talked about them in our previous activities. If a person has these qualities, we say that he or she has a godly character.

As Christians, we should be trying to develop the fruit of the Spirit in our lives. The Holy Spirit is the one who develops these character traits in us. Let's do an activity to help us understand this.

Pour about an inch of milk into an 11"×13½" pan. Gather students around the pan.

Let's say that this pan of milk represents your life. These food-coloring drops are good character traits in our life. I will choose one person to add a drop of coloring into the milk. As you drop it in, name one good character trait that we should have. **Let five or six students drop drops and name a character trait mentioned in Galatians 5:22,23.**

Doesn't the milk look pretty now? That's the way our lives seem to others when we display the fruits of the Spirit.

- Who is the only Person who can put these good character traits into our lives? *(The Holy Spirit.)*

Without the Holy Spirit's work in our lives, we wouldn't have the desire or ability to do these things. God helps us build new character traits in our lives that take the place of the old sinful ones.

Now let's say this knife represents the Holy Spirit's work in us. **Hold up the knife.** As He comes into our lives, He makes sure all these good traits become even more beautiful.

Swirl the knife through the colors to create a beautiful rainbow effect. (Caution: Too much swirling will make it brown!)

The fruits of the Spirit prove that we are letting the Holy Spirit control our lives. We will produce the spiritual fruit that we let Him grow in our lives. If we do wrong things, we become like thorny weeds to people around us. If we let the Holy Spirit work in us, we will produce sweet fruit like grapes or oranges or pineapple.

- How does it feel when you produce the thorny weeds of bad deeds in your life? *(It makes me feel guilty. I get into trouble and that feels bad.)*

- How does it feel when you develop good character traits in your life? *(Happy; glad; I have less stress.)*

- How do you think character traits like patience, love, peace, and the other fruits of the Holy Spirit combine to make a more beautiful rainbow in our lives? *(When we have one of them, it makes the other ones better. One good character trait helps us want to have others.)*

The New Testament is full of examples of people who allowed the Holy Spirit to make rainbows of good characteristics in their lives that others could see. We read about Stephen. Peter healed people in the power of the Holy Spirit. Paul told people about Jesus even when he was beaten or put into prison for doing this. Only the Holy Spirit can produce spiritual fruit in our lives.

MEMORY VERSE ACTIVITY: Fruit Basket Upset

Ephesians 5:18—"Do not get drunk on wine, which leads to debauchery. Instead, be filled with the Spirit."

Let's learn a memory verse that will help us remember to ask to be filled with the Holy Spirit.

Lead your group in reciting Ephesians 5:18 several times. Privately, assign each student the name of one of the fruits of the Spirit. Then arrange chairs in a circle. Select one person to be in the center, and remove that person's chair. Have the person in the center call out two or more fruits of the Spirit. Those students, including the person in the center, have to find a new chair. The one who ends up without a chair becomes the new person in the center. That person must first recite the verse, then call out the names of spiritual fruit. Repeat the game until everyone has had a chance to say the verse. Then recite the verse together as a group.

WEEKLY ASSIGNMENT: Spiritual Fruit Basket

Distribute the "Spiritual Fruit Basket" handouts. This week, let's see how many fruits of the Spirit others can see in your life. When you get home, cut out the fruit basket and the fruit. Color them if you like. Each day, ask God to fill you with His Holy Spirit. Then look for ways to obey God. When you get into a situation where you display one of the fruits of the Spirit, remember it. Then when you have time, write the name of that spiritual fruit on the front of one of the fruit pictures. Write about or draw the situation on the back of your fruit. Put that fruit in your basket. For example, if you were kind to someone who called you a bad name, you kept the peace. Write "peace" on a fruit and explain what happened on the back of the fruit picture. Put it in your basket. See if you can get all of your fruit into your basket.

Close in prayer, asking God to help you and your students consistently display the fruits of the Spirit in your lives.

Life Circles

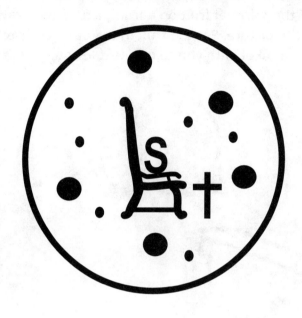

jealousy

worry

being discouraged

swearing

lying

cheating

gossiping

disobeying parents

not praying

not reading the Bible

love

joy

peace

patience

kindness

faithfulness

goodness

prays

obeys God

tells others about Jesus

Spiritual Fruit Basket

Cut out the basket and the fruit. Cut on the dotted line in the center of the basket. Each day this week, ask God to fill you with His Holy Spirit. Then, each time you display one of the fruits of the Spirit (love, joy, peace, patience, kindness, goodness, faithfulness, gentleness, and self-control), write the name of the spiritual fruit on a fruit picture and draw or write about the situation on the back of the picture. Put the fruit in the basket. Try to get all of your fruit into your basket. Bring the basket with you to our next lesson.

Walking in the Spirit

LESSON PLAN

OBJECTIVE: Students will learn how to practice walking in the Spirit daily.

APPLICATION: Students will begin practicing Spiritual Breathing.

LESSON PLAN ELEMENT	ACTIVITY	TIME	SUPPLIES
Opening Activity	*Disconnected Dominoes*	7–10	At least two sets of dominoes; dead branch; Bible
Bible Story—John 15:1–17, the Vine and the Branches	*Sweet or Sour*	10–15	Healthy plant or tree branch; dead branch; pruning shears or scissors; small paper cups; grape juice; vinegar; Bible
Lesson Activity	*Good Grapes*	9–10	A weed that grows as a vine, such as Creeping Charlie
Application	*Five Footprints*	5–10	Construction paper; pencils
Memory Verse Activity	*The Verse Vine*	3–5	Balloons
Check for Understanding	*Changing Circles*	3–5	Dry-erase marker or chalk
Weekly Assignment	*Good Grapes Rule!*	3–5	"Good Grapes Rule!" handouts

When you purchase a mechanical item that runs on battery power, frequently the notice "Batteries Not Included" is printed on the box. The Holy Spirit, your Source of power for living, is "included" when you receive Jesus Christ as your Savior and Lord. Therefore, you do not need to invite Him to come into your life. He came to live within you when you became a Christian, and Jesus promised that He will never leave you (Hebrews 13:5).

The moment we received Christ, the Holy Spirit came to indwell us to give us spiritual life, causing us to be born anew as a child of God. The Holy Spirit also baptizes each believer into the body of Christ (1 Corinthians 12:13). Therefore, there is but one indwelling of the Holy Spirit, one rebirth of the Holy Spirit, one baptism of the Holy Spirit—all of which occur when you receive Christ.

Being filled with the Holy Spirit, however, is not a once-for-all experience. There are many fillings, as is made clear in Ephesians 5:18. In this lesson, your students will learn how to be continually filled with the Holy Spirit as a way of life.

To explain the concept of being continually filled with the Holy Spirit, we can use an example called Spiritual Breathing. As believers, we can "exhale" the impure through confessing our sin and "inhale" the pure by asking to be filled with God's Holy Spirit. By practicing Spiritual Breathing on a consistent basis, your students can learn to walk step-by-step with God to overcome temptation, to minister to others, and to experience the joy that God intends for us to have.

By teaching your young students this concept, you will prepare them for the many trials they will encounter as teenagers and adults. This is practical Christian living that works! As you prepare for this lesson, practice Spiritual Breathing in your own life. Then plan to tell your students how walking in the Spirit has made your life richer and your relationship with God more intimate.

LESSON PLAN

OPENING ACTIVITY: Disconnected Dominoes

To begin, allow students to share what they have written or drawn on the fruits in their fruit basket. Encourage them to describe how they felt when they produced good fruit with the help of the Holy Spirit.

Divide the class into three or four groups. Give each group some dominoes. Let's begin by doing something fun. In your groups, make an interesting domino chain. Once you get it set up, we will watch the chain reaction as your dominoes fall in order together. I will give you 5 minutes to make your chain. **Give students time to assemble their domino chains. When finished, gather in a large group.**

Let's watch group 1 set off their domino chain. **Have the students watch as the chain works.** Isn't that fun? It's exciting to see all those dominoes work together in a connected chain!

Now let's watch group 2 as they set off their chain reaction. But before we do, I am going to take out one domino. **Remove a key domino so that the chain will stop in the middle.** Okay, let's start the chain.

When the chain stops, hold up the missing domino. This missing domino caused the chain to disconnect. This made it less exciting to watch because the chain didn't work the way it was supposed to.

Let's watch as group 3 sets off their domino chain. But first, I am going to take out one domino. **Remove a domino that's very close to the front of the chain.** Okay, let's start the chain. **The chain will stop right away. When the chain stops, hold up the missing domino.** This missing domino caused the chain to mess up right at the beginning. The chain is completed disconnected.

If you have a fourth group, let them set off their chain without taking out a domino. Again, remark on the well-working chain and the beauty of its togetherness. Let groups 2 and 3 replace their missing dominoes and reset their fallen dominoes, and then watch their chain reactions.

Read John 15:5. This verse explains how we are connected to Jesus Christ in our daily life. In John 15:5, Jesus calls Himself the vine. **Hold up the dead branch.** Jesus says that we are like branches. If a branch isn't connected to the living vine, it is useless. It can do nothing. Just like the disconnected dominoes could do nothing, so Christians can do nothing unless they are connected to Jesus Christ. They become like the disconnected domino chains. Let's listen to our Bible story to see how this works.

BIBLE STORY: Sweet or Sour

Before Class: Set out the healthy plant or tree branch, dead branch, and pruning shears or scissors. Pour small amounts of grape juice and vinegar in small paper cups so that each student has one of each.

Instruct students to sit around a table. I have given each of you a small cup of vinegar and a small cup of grape juice. They are opposites of each other. Keep them in front of you because we will do things with them as today's lesson unfolds.

Our lesson today comes from John 15. Jesus and His disciples had just finished eating the Last Supper. Jesus knew He would soon die and leave His disciples. He explains that He is going to die within the next few days and tells them that He will send the Holy Spirit in His place. He also tells them many things about how to live the Christian life after He is gone. One example He gave was of the vine and the branches. These verses help us understand how to walk in the Spirit. Let's look closely at John 15 and see what Jesus had to say.

Jesus refers to Himself as the true vine and God the Father as the gardener or vinedresser. In Jesus' time, vineyards or grape fields were everywhere. People knew the basics of keeping up a vineyard, so His example of a vine made sense to them. **Read John 15:1–3.**

Hold up the healthy plant you brought in. When Jesus talked about the vine, He was referring to a healthy plant like this. We'll let this plant represent the true vine of Jesus.

Point out a small branch on the plant. Jesus said we are like branches that grow from the vine. Each branch was supposed to produce a bunch of grapes. The vinedresser carefully watched each vine. If a branch didn't produce any grapes, the gardener would cut it away. **Snip a small branch off your plant.** If branches were producing grapes, the gardener would prune or cut it back a little. This helps the branch produce even more fruit. **Snip a leaf or two off a thick branch from your plant.**

Read John 15:4–7. Jesus told His disciples that a branch cannot produce fruit on its own. **Hold up the branch that you snipped off.** This branch will never have life again to enable it to produce fruit. It needs to be connected to the vine. Branches that are cut off dry up. **Hold up the dead branch.** This branch is only good for firewood or to be thrown away.

Let's look at the fruit of the vine. Grapes are produced by branches that are connected to the vine. Smell your cup of grape juice. It's a sweet smell. Dip your finger in and taste it. It's a sweet taste.

Now take the other cup. This represents what happens if the branch produces bad fruit. Smell the vinegar. It's made from fruit, too, but it has a sour smell. A rotting branch would give off a similar smell. Dip your finger in and taste it. It's a sour taste. A rotting branch would have a similar taste.

Jesus said that we should be like the healthy branch that was connected to the vine and produced fruit. He called this "remaining in Him." When we remain in Jesus, we produce spiritual fruit. **Read John 15:8.**

Remember the spiritual fruit we learned about in our last lesson? **Read Galatians 5:22,23.** Jesus told His disciples several ways that they could abide in Him to produce spiritual fruit.

One way was to keep His commandments. The Holy Spirit helps us do this by helping us resist temptation. **Read John 15:9–11,14.**

Another way was to love one another. The Holy Spirit can fill us with Christ's love so that we can love others—even people who are hard to love. **Read John 15:12.**

Another way we can produce fruit is by telling others about Jesus. We are to follow Jesus' example. **Read John 15:15.**

As Christians we should remain in Jesus Christ. We should produce good fruit. **Read John 15:16,17.**

- How do you think producing spiritual fruit will make you feel? *(Like I'm doing something good; closer to God.)*

- Why do you think producing spiritual fruit is so important? *(God told us to do it. We are better people when we do it.)*

- Think of someone you know who produces lots of spiritual fruit. What about his or her life do you admire? *(He is kind. She keeps her promises. He doesn't cause fights.)*

Smell the sweet smell of the grape juice again. Smell the vinegar. Are you connected to Jesus Christ? Are you abiding in the vine or have you cut yourself off from the Holy Spirit's work in your life? In our Lesson Activity, we'll discover how we can abide in the Spirit in our daily life.

LESSON ACTIVITY: Good Grapes

Display the noxious vine (weed) you brought.

We've been talking about being connected to the vine, Jesus Christ. That's how we produce spiritual fruit. But something can come in and choke off all the fruit you produce.

Hold up the weed. This is a vine that we call a weed. It grows everywhere, especially in places where it's not wanted, like a garden or a lawn. Once this weed gets a good start, it kills everything else in the garden. It takes all the water and nutrients from the soil. It grows around the good plants until it chokes them to death. If this weed is not pulled out by the roots, it will take over the garden and you will not have any fruit. This weed is called Creeping Charlie.

We have many Creeping Charlies in our life too. They are things like lying, breaking promises, swearing, being sneaky, watching bad videos. In other words, the Creeping Charlie in our lives is sin.

- Think of a time when you started doing something you knew was wrong and it got out of hand. How did it feel? *(Allow students to describe their experiences. Guide them in telling how their sin was making their lives difficult.)*

- How was your experience like a Creeping Charlie choking out plants in a garden? *(It choked all the fun out of what I was doing. I got into worse and worse trouble.)*

It's hard to do what's right. It's hard for children. It's hard for teenagers. And it's hard for adults. But God has given us a way to say "no" to temptation so we won't sin. That way is by asking the Holy Spirit to help us.

In our last lesson, we learned how important it is to be filled with the Holy Spirit. That is the secret to producing spiritual fruit. But how can we remember to ask God to fill us with His Spirit all the time and to forgive us of our sin? We can do something called Spiritual Breathing.

- How does breathing work? *(We suck in good air and blow out bad air. We take air in and out to get oxygen to our body.)*

- What would happen if we kept taking air in and never breathed out? *(We'd get too full of air. The bad air would stay in our lungs and poison us.)*

When we breathe, we exhale or breathe out all the bad air. Then we inhale or breathe in good, fresh air. The bad air contains carbon dioxide that would poison us if we kept it inside. The good air contains oxygen that our body needs to survive and grow.

Together, let's breathe. First, breathe out. **Pause for students to do this.** Now breathe in. **Pause for students to do this.** When you're playing or studying, do you have to work hard to breathe? No, you do it naturally. That's what we want to do when we do Spiritual Breathing. We want it to become so natural that we do it all the time.

This is how Spiritual Breathing works. Breathing out means getting the bad out of our lives or confessing our sin. **Read 1 John 1:9.** This is the exhaling part of Spiritual Breathing. Then we inhale the good. The good we inhale is being filled with the Holy Spirit. **Read Ephesians 5:18.** The Holy Spirit is perfect and pure, like fresh air. He helps us do what is good.

- What would happen if we tried to inhale the Holy Spirit before we exhaled by confessing our sin? *(It wouldn't work because we would still be full of bad things. The sin would get in the way of the Holy Spirit.)*

Remember how we decided that sin would choke our lives like the Creeping Charlie chokes good plants? The same principle is true for Spiritual Breathing. If we don't confess our sins, they will crowd out the Holy Spirit's work in our lives. We need to get rid of the sin so the Holy Spirit can be free to work.

This is how it works in real life. Chad has a problem with swearing. He tries to quit, but every time he gets in a tight spot, those bad words just come out before he can stop them.

- What does he need to do first? *(Exhale by confessing to God that his swearing is sin.)*

When he does this, he cleans his heart attitude to open it up for the Holy Spirit to work. Remember, the Holy Spirit is always in your life. From the moment you asked Jesus to be your Savior, the Holy Spirit lives in you. But the Holy Spirit can't work in your life if it is full of sin.

- What should Chad do next? *(He should ask the Holy Spirit to fill him and help him stop swearing.)*

The next thing Chad should do is to inhale the good—ask God to fill him with the Holy Spirit. Then Chad should let the Holy Spirit do the work in helping him to stop swearing.

- What happens if Chad messes up and swears again? *(He should do Spiritual Breathing all over again.)*

God wants us to confess our sin to him each time we do wrong. We can ask to be filled with the Holy Spirit any time we want to be filled. Let me read a verse that shows how God keeps His promises. **Read 1 John 5:14,15.**

This verse says we can be sure that God will give us whatever we know is in His will for us. God commands us to be filled with the Holy Spirit. That means that He wants us to be filled with the Spirit at all times. It is His will. In this verse, He promises to help us do whatever He commands us to do. He doesn't just give us a rule and then expect us to do it by ourselves. He helps us follow His commands.

When we practice Spiritual Breathing every day, every hour, sometimes even every minute, we will be allowing the Holy Spirit to do His work in our lives. We will produce lots of spiritual fruit. We will stay connected to Jesus, our vine. We call this kind of life "walking with the Holy Spirit."

- What situations do you face in which you need to practice Spiritual Breathing? *(When my little sister bugs me. When I don't feel like doing my homework. When someone calls me names.)*

- How do you think Spiritual Breathing will help you in those situations? *(I can be kind to my little sister even when I don't feel like it. I will get my homework done on time and even have more time to play. I can love someone who calls me names instead of calling names back.)*

Spiritual Breathing is just part of abiding in Christ. How can we stay connected to Him? Let's look at five ways we can do just that.

APPLICATION: Five Footprints

Many people never think about how to live a life that includes God in every moment. But we can! God wants us to walk in His Spirit every moment of every day. Five action points will help us do this. Let's think about them as five footprints for walking in the Spirit.

Distribute paper and pencils. Have students draw five shoe prints on their papers. As you discuss each point, draw a shoe print on the board and write the point in a print. Have students do the same, writing each point in a shoe print as you discuss it. Then think of ways to apply each action point. A few examples are given for each action point. Encourage students to jot down ways they can do that action point in their daily lives.

1. Love God with all your heart.

   (Each day, tell God you love Him.)

   (Make sure God is more important than things like your bike, your video games, or your friends. Ask Him to give you more love for Him.)

   (Write a prayer of love to God.)

2. Practice Spiritual Breathing.

   (Confess sin as soon as you recognize you have done wrong.)

   (Then ask God to fill you with His Holy Spirit.)

3. Spend time daily in prayer and Bible study.

   (Instead of reading the cereal box at breakfast, read a verse in your Bible and pray.)

   (Put a card with a Bible verse in your backpack to read it during lunch at school and pray silently about it.)

   (Use a children's Bible to study about Jesus and His disciples.)

4. Obey God's commands.

   (Memorize the Ten Commandments in Exodus 20 and follow them.)

   (Listen to your Bible lessons in church and do what you learn that week.)

5. Witness for Christ.

   (Ask God to help you tell others about Jesus.)

   (Explain to your friends how much God loves them and that Jesus died for their sins.)

   (Invite your friends to church.)

Take your footprint papers home to help remind you of ways to walk in the Spirit. Perhaps you would like to cut out the footprints and "walk" them over your bedroom walls.

MEMORY VERSE ACTIVITY: The Verse Vine

John 15:4—"Remain in Me, and I will remain in you. No branch can bear fruit by itself; it must remain in the vine. Neither can you bear fruit unless you remain in Me."

Write the verse on the chalkboard. Read the verse to the students, then lead the students in reading the verse together several times. Discuss how we must be connected to Jesus to produce fruit and walk in the Spirit.

Have the students stand. Divide into groups of four or five students and give each group a balloon. Each group is a vine, so you must be connected to each person in your group by holding hands or by touching shoulders, knees, or feet. **Have groups practice the verse by volleying the balloon back and forth. With every hit of the balloon, that person should say the next word of the verse. Tell students that they will soon be competing against the other groups. Give groups a few minutes to practice.**

DISCOVERING OUR AWESOME GOD

Teaching Tip: If your students have problems holding hands with a student of the opposite sex, form groups of all boys and all girls.

Remember in our story we talked about how we need to be connected to Jesus, the true vine. Each group is a vine and the balloon is the fruit. Your goal is to keep the fruit off the ground for the longest time. You can hit the balloon with any part of your body, but the vine must always be connected. The person who hits the balloon must also say the next word in the verse. As a group, you can help the person by prompting him or her. If the wrong word is said or the balloon hits the ground, your group is out. Sit down and wait for the other groups to finish. The last group remaining will be the winner.

Try this activity several times. Then have the groups practice saying the verse while sitting in a circle.

CHECK FOR UNDERSTANDING: Changing Circles
You will be drawing the following diagram on the chalkboard or white board:

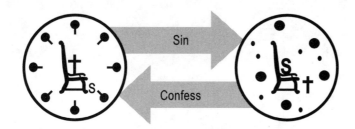

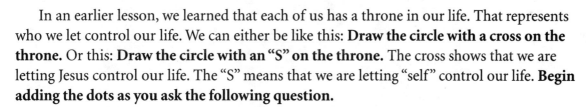

In an earlier lesson, we learned that each of us has a throne in our life. That represents who we let control our life. We can either be like this: **Draw the circle with a cross on the throne.** Or this: **Draw the circle with an "S" on the throne.** The cross shows that we are letting Jesus control our life. The "S" means that we are letting "self" control our life. **Begin adding the dots as you ask the following question.**

• What qualities are true of someone who lets Jesus control his life? *(Allow students to give answers such as: love, joy, peace, gentleness, prayer, kindness, self-control, patience.)*

Draw eight dots in an orderly fashion around the throne.

• What about the life where self is in control? What qualities are true of someone like this? *(Allow students to give answers such as: is unkind, picks fights, swears, is mean, doesn't pray, is selfish, is impatient, acts proud.)*

Draw eight dots in random order around the throne.

All of us act like each of these circles at times in our lives. How does Spiritual Breathing help? If you found yourself putting "self" on the throne, what would you do?

Help students explain the process of Spiritual Breathing. As they do, draw the arrows between the circles and label them "Sin" and "Confess."

WEEKLY ASSIGNMENT: Good Grapes Rule!
Distribute the "Good Grapes" handouts.

We can also use a branch drawing to help us to remember to practice Spiritual Breathing every day. This week, let's see how many good bunches of grapes you can put on your branch. Then you can say, "Good Grapes Rule!"

When you get home, cut out the Branch picture, Creeping Charlie vines, and the Good Grapes bunches. Attach the Branch on your bulletin board or refrigerator. Tape the Creeping Charlie onto the Branch so it looks like the Branch is being swallowed by the weeds.

Each time you encounter a situation where you practiced Spiritual Breathing, take off one Creeping Charlie and tape up one bunch of Good Grapes in its place. See if you can replace all the Creeping Charlie with Good Grapes. When you do, replace all the grapes with Creeping Charlie and try it all over again. The goal is to practice Spiritual Breathing each time you find yourself tempted to sin or in a situation where you need the Holy Spirit's help.

Close in prayer, asking God to help your students remember to practice Spiritual Breathing this week.

Good Grapes

Cut out the drawings. Put the Branch on your bulletin board or refrigerator. Tape the Creeping Charlie vines to the Branch. Each time you encounter a situation where you practiced Spiritual Breathing, take off one Creeping Charlie and tape up one bunch of Good Grapes in its place. See if you can replace all the Creeping Charlie with Good Grapes. If you do, replace all the grapes with Creeping Charlie and try it all over again. The goal is to practice Spiritual Breathing each time you find yourself tempted to sin or in a situation where you need the Holy Spirit's help.

What Is Prayer?

BOOK OBJECTIVE	To introduce students to God and help them understand His nature.
UNIT OBJECTIVE	To encourage students to develop a lifestyle of communicating with God.
LESSON 9: Purposes for Prayer	*Objective:* To help students understand the purposes of prayer and to whom they should pray.
	Application: To encourage students to pray for each other using the purposes of prayer.
LESSON 10: Plan for Prayer	*Objective:* To help students learn how to apply a simple guide to a daily prayer time.
	Application: To encourage students to use the ACTS method of prayer.
LESSON 11: Power in Prayer	*Objective:* To help students learn how to claim by faith the great power available through prevailing prayer.
	Application: To encourage students to prevail in prayer through a daily prayer plan.
LESSON 12: Promises for Prayer	*Objective:* To help students learn how to claim God's promises in prayer.
	Application: To help students plan a definite place, time, and activities for spending time with God and for claiming promises from Scripture in their prayers.
LESSON 13: Trinity Triangle	*Objective:* To help students learn how the members of the Trinity work together to accomplish God's work.
	Application: To encourage students to pray consistently to the Father, in the power of the Spirit, and in Jesus' name.

A story is told of a man who traveled to a certain city one cold morning. As he arrived at his hotel, he noticed that the clerks, the guests—everyone—were barefoot. In the coffee shop, he noticed an attractive fellow at a nearby table and asked, "Why aren't you wearing shoes? Don't you know about shoes?"

"Of course I know about shoes," the patron replied.

"Then why don't you wear them?" the visitor asked.

"Ah, that is the question," the patron returned. "Why don't I wear shoes?"

After breakfast, the visitor walked out of the hotel and into the snow. Again, every person he saw was barefoot. Curious, he asked a passerby, "Why doesn't anyone here wear shoes? Don't you know that they protect the feet from the cold?"

The passerby said, "We know about shoes. See that building? It's a shoe factory. We are so proud of the plant that we gather there every week to hear the man in charge tell us how wonderful shoes are."

"Then why don't you wear shoes?" the visitor persisted.

"Ah, that is the question," the passerby replied. "Why don't we wear shoes?"

When it comes to prayer, many Christians are like the people in that city. They know about prayer; they believe in its power; they frequently hear sermons on the subject; but prayer is not a vital part of their lives.

Wherever people really pray according to biblical principles, God works in their lives and through them in the lives of others in a special way. Any Christian who emphasizes prayer will consequently have a ministry where people are excited about Jesus Christ and will be living and witnessing for Him. On the other hand, a believer who has little emphasis on prayer is a worldly Christian who has little interest in the souls of men and women. The lives of these worldly believers can best be described by the experience of the church of Ephesus in Revelation 2 and the church of Laodicea in Revelation 3.

Our power does not lie in money, genius, or dedicated work, but in prayer. E. M. Bounds writes:

> The Church is looking for better methods; God is looking for better men ... What the Church needs today is not more or better machinery, not new organizations or more and novel methods, but men whom the Holy Ghost can use—men of prayer, men mighty in prayer. The Holy Ghost does not flow through methods, but through men. He does not come on machinery, but on men. He does not anoint plans, but men—men of prayer.

The worldwide Church is only as faithful as its next generation. If our children do not grasp the significance of prayer, the power of prayer, and the purpose for prayer, they will not be able to enter the future in victory. These youngsters not only need to understand what prayer is, but they need to be given models of adults who pray and a plan to implement prayer in their lives.

As you carefully teach the following lessons, it is our sincere desire that you will see the importance of prayer and that you will begin immediately to apply prayer in your life and to model effective prayer before your students.

Purposes for Prayer

LESSON PLAN

OBJECTIVE: Students will understand the purposes of prayer and to whom they should pray.

APPLICATION: Students will pray for each other using the purposes of prayer.

LESSON PLAN ELEMENT	ACTIVITY	TIME	SUPPLIES
Opening Activity	*Powerful Prayers*	5–10	11-foot pieces of string; straws; balloons; tape; chairs; black markers
Bible Story—Acts 3 and 4, Peter and John imprisoned	*All Shook Up*	8–10	Chalk or dry-erase marker; can of warm soda; several copies of the "All Shook Up" handout; pencils; scissors; Bible; tape
Lesson Activity	*Purposeful Prayers*	8–10	Chalk or dry-erase markers; 6 empty one-liter bottles; vinegar; 6 balloons; 6 paper cups; baking soda; flour; tablespoon; measuring cup; black marker
Application	*Circles of Prayer*	10–15	Masking tape; inflated balloon; timer; chalk or dry-erase marker; Bible; slips of paper; pencils
Weekly Assignment	*Prayer Balloons*	1–2	Balloons; slips of paper from previous activity; tape
Check for Understanding	*Pop the Question*	3–5	6 balloons; 6 slips of paper; pen
Memory Verse Activity	*Balloon Bust*	5–8	12 balloons; 12 small slips of paper; 1 pin; dry-erase marker or chalk; eraser

LESSON INTRODUCTION

What is prayer? Simply put, prayer is communicating with God. As a child of God, you are invited to come boldly before His throne. "Since we have a great high priest who has gone through the heavens, Jesus the Son of God," the apostle Paul writes, "...let us then approach the throne of grace with confidence, so that we may receive mercy and find grace to help us in our time of need" (Hebrews 4:14–16).

Because of who God is—the King of kings and the Lord of lords, the Creator of heaven and earth—we must come into His presence with reverence. But He is also our loving heavenly Father who cares for us and delights in having fellowship with us. Therefore, we can come to Him with a reverent, joyful heart, knowing He loves us more than anyone else has ever loved us or will ever love us.

Someone has said, "Prayer is the creator as well as the channel of devotion. The spirit of devotion is prayer. Prayer and devotion are united as soul and body are united, as life and heart are united. There is no prayer without devotion, no devotion without prayer." Real prayer is expressing our devotion to our heavenly Father, inviting Him to talk to us as we talk to Him.

Jesus set the perfect example of obedience in prayer. Although His day was filled from morning to night with many pressures and responsibilities—addressing crowds, healing the sick, granting private interviews, traveling, and training His disciples—He made prayer a top priority. If Jesus was so dependent upon fellowship alone with His Father, how much more you and I should spend time alone with God.

The lives of the disciples and other Christians who have been mightily used by God through the centuries to reach their world for Christ all testify to the necessity of prayer. They too are examples of obedience to our Lord's command to pray.

Someone has wisely said, "Satan laughs at our toiling, mocks at our wisdom, but trembles when he sees the weakest saint on his knees." Prayer is God's appointed way of doing God's work.

So far, your students have learned about the magnificent character of God and how much He loves each of us. They have learned how to walk in the power of the Holy Spirit to become more like Jesus. To culminate all this knowledge, this unit, "What Is Prayer?" will show your students how they can pray effectively to build an intimate relationship with God. This lesson will help them understand why prayer is so important to our Christian life.

OPENING ACTIVITY: Powerful Prayers

So far, we have discovered how awesome God really is. We have also learned how the Holy Spirit helps us live the Christian life. **Ask:**

- What is prayer? *(Talking to God.)*

- Did you know that some prayers are more powerful than others? Can you think of why? *(A person who has known God longer can pray better; adults can pray better; some people know how to pray right.)*

Surprisingly, many of us think those are some of the reasons why people have an exciting prayer life. But we must go by what God says about prayer. Let me read John 15:7, where Jesus said, "If you remain in Me and My words remain in you, ask whatever you wish, and it will be given you." The key to effective prayer goes back to our depending on Jesus for strength, power, and ability. Let's do an activity to understand what this means.

Divide students into four or five groups. Have each group place two chairs 8 to 10 feet apart. Give each group one piece of string, one straw, one balloon, tape, and a black marker. Tie one end of your string to one of the chairs. Thread your string through the straw and tie the other end to the other chair. Move the straw to one end. Blow up your balloon one-quarter of the way, but don't tie it. This balloon represents a person who relies on his own power to solve problems. He spends little  time talking to God or reading His Word. This person doesn't get much power from God. Now tape the balloon onto the straw and let the balloon go. Mark the string where the balloon stops. **Give students time to do this part of the activity.**

Blow the balloon up again, but this time fill it full. This balloon represents a Christian who relies on the Lord moment by moment. He allows God's Word to fill him up and he reads the Bible and prays daily. He immediately turns to God for help in every situation. Now, without tying the balloon, tape it to the straw and let the balloon go. **Give groups time to complete this part of the activity.**

- Did the balloon go past the old mark? *(Yes.)*

- Why? *(The first balloon didn't have enough power. The second balloon had more air to push it farther.)*

- How is the balloon with more power like the person who prays? *(The person who prays has God's power. Prayer can take us farther.)*

The person who relies on God and abides in Him will be able to ask God for anything. His prayers will be very powerful. This person will be filled with the Holy Spirit, who will help him do what's right.

Let's listen to a story from the Bible that tells of a time when powerful prayers were spoken.

BIBLE STORY: All Shook Up

Before Class: Draw a large soda can on the board. The can should be big enough so that the "foam" pieces on the "All Shook Up" handout will fit on the top. Label the soda can "Powerade." Cut apart the "foam" pieces from the handout.

I want to give you an important statement. *Prayer is one of the most powerful activities a person can do.* That's because when we pray, we bring our problem to God for His help. And God is more powerful than anything in the universe.

Prayer is communicating with God. When we pray, we talk to our heavenly Father. He listens to us because He loves us. He sees what we need and He answers our prayer. He answers using His strength, power, and wisdom. As we pray, we learn more about Him and grow closer to Him. **Hold up the can of soda.**

- What would happen if I shook up this warm soda can and opened it? (*It would foam over. Soda would get all over everything.*)

Prayer shakes things up. It makes things happen. Let's look at what can happen when prayer shakes things up.

Give each person a pencil, scissors, and one piece of "foam" from the "All Shook Up" handout. I am going to read a story from Acts chapter 4. As I read it, write down at least one thing that happened when the people in the story prayed.

Open your Bible to Acts 4:1–31. Read the following story slowly, giving students time to write. Suggestions for answers to prayer are underlined. You may help your students by giving the first answer as an idea.

Peter and John were very excited about telling others about Jesus. They were excited about the fact that Jesus had died and risen again. And they had seen Him alive! The more they preached about Jesus, the more people believed in Him and became Christians. One day, when Peter and John were going to the temple to pray, they met a man who couldn't walk. Peter and John healed the man and he could walk immediately! <u>Peter and John healed in the power of God as they walked and talked with God.</u>

People who saw what had happened were amazed. <u>Many people believed in Jesus because of what Peter and John had done through the power of God and prayer.</u>

The religious rulers didn't like what Peter and John were doing. They were jealous of what God was doing through the two apostles. These rulers grabbed Peter and John and threw them in jail. <u>I'm sure that Peter and John were praying while they were in jail like they did on other occasions.</u> God kept them safe. The next day, the rulers met in Jerusalem and they questioned Peter and John. "By what power did you heal this man?" they demanded. Peter answered, "It was through the power of the name of Jesus!" <u>Peter and John had prayed in Jesus' name.</u>

The rulers were amazed at what Peter and John had done because the apostles had never gone to school; they had learned all they knew from Jesus. The rulers were afraid of Peter and John because the people thought they were great. So the rulers told Peter and John to quit talking about Jesus. But Peter and John were brave. <u>Their prayer helped them rely on the power of God.</u> They told the rulers that they would not stop telling everyone about Jesus. They would obey God rather than the rulers.

<u>The rulers let Peter and John go because all the people were praising God for what He had done through the two men.</u>

As soon as they were released, Peter and John went back to their own people and told them all that had happened. Together, they all prayed, exclaiming about all the things that God had done.

<u>After they had prayed, the whole place where they were meeting was shaken, almost as if an earthquake had happened. All the people were filled with the Holy Spirit and they all told about God's Word with boldness.</u>

Can you imagine what that was like? It was as if the place was shaken like a can of soda and everything burst out. Everyone talked about Jesus.

Let's take our "foam" pieces and put them on the Powerade soda can I've drawn on the board to show how prayer shakes things up. **Have students come up one at a time and tape their "foam" pieces to the top of the can, telling what they wrote on their "foam." Bring out each underlined point in the story.**

- What amazes you most about the power of prayer? *(That God would listen to me. That God will do miracles.)*

- How does it make you feel when God answers one of your prayers? *(Like God really loves me. Like God is watching over me.)*

God didn't take away all of Peter and John's problems. They still ended up in jail and had to appear before the religious rulers who hated them. But God worked through the problems when the people prayed.

Many times people get confused about what prayer is all about. Let's see what God's Word says about the purpose of prayer.

LESSON ACTIVITY: Purposeful Prayers

 Before Class: Fill the six paper cups with four or five tablespoons of the following materials and label as shown:

3 cups with baking soda, with the labels:

to glorify God

to ask God to supply what we need

to desire to talk to God and praise Him

3 cups with flour, with the labels:

to look good or impress others

to selfishly ask for things we want but do not need

because others want us to pray but we don't want to

Make sure the amounts of flour and baking soda in each cup are the same. Put about a cup of vinegar in each of the one-liter bottles. Set the bottles on a demonstration table with the labeled cups, balloons, and the spoon set to the side.

Have students sit near the demonstration table. Think for a moment of reasons why you pray. Let's list some of them. **Write the students' ideas on the board.** Very often, we think of praying only at times when we need something or when we are in trouble. But the Bible tells us that there are some definite reasons we should pray. Let's look at a demonstration to understand this more.

Point out the six one-liter bottles. Say, Let's have these six bottles represent our prayers. As we pray, we often have different reasons or purposes. **Point out the material in the cups.** When people pray, their prayers can sound alike, just like the white material in these cups looks alike. But God looks at our hearts, at our heart attitude. He knows what our prayers are made of. That makes a big difference in what happens when we pray. Let's see what some of these reasons or purposes should or should not be.

Read Matthew 6:5. In this verse, Jesus is talking about people who pray to look good to others. Their hearts aren't really in what they are praying. Sometimes, we also pray to impress others.

Take the cup of flour labeled "to look good or impress others" and scoop the flour into a balloon. Put the lip of the balloon over the first bottle, letting the balloon flop over so that the flour cannot drop into the bottle. If we pray with this purpose, God says that our prayers are worthless. They will not be effective or accomplish anything. **Tip up the balloon so that all the flour drops into the vinegar. (You may have to gently shake the balloon.)** Notice how nothing happened to our balloon. It is still just as flat as before.

Read John 14:13. This verse tells us that we should pray to bring glory to God. **Scoop baking soda from cup labeled "to glorify God" and place it into the second balloon. Put the balloon lip over the second bottle and shake the balloon until the soda falls into the bottle. There will be a gas reaction when the soda hits the vinegar, making the balloon**

inflate slightly. Notice that this time the balloon has blown up. If we pray with the purpose of glorifying God, our prayers are effective and will accomplish something.

Sometimes we pray to get things we want because we are selfish. **Read James 4:3.** These things could be more toys, money, or other possessions. **Scoop flour from the cup labeled "to selfishly ask for things we want but do not need" into the third balloon. Put the balloon lip over the third bottle. Nothing will happen to the balloon.** If we pray just to get something, our prayers are worthless. They have no power. Notice that again nothing happened to the balloon.

Let's read what the Bible says our purpose should be. **Read Matthew 7:7.** We don't need to be afraid to ask God for things He wants us to have, things He knows we need or that are good for us. **Scoop baking soda from the cup labeled "to ask God to supply what we need" into the fourth balloon. Put the balloon lip over the fourth bottle so that the baking soda falls into the vinegar. Again, the balloon will get larger.** Notice the reaction to our prayer when we ask God to supply what we need. God is very willing to give us things He knows are good for us and that we need.

Sometimes we pray because others want us to. We really don't desire to do it ourselves. Maybe your mom or dad makes you say your prayers before going to bed or you are forced to pray in a group but your heart is not in it. Let's see how effective this type of prayer is. **Scoop flour from the cup labeled "because others want us to pray but we don't want to" into the fifth balloon and put the balloon lip over the fifth bottle. Shake the flour into the vinegar. No reaction will occur.** If we pray with this purpose, our prayers are worthless and don't accomplish anything. Notice that again nothing happened to the balloon. When someone asks us to pray, we need to get our heart right and want to pray rather than just saying the words. We also shouldn't refuse to pray because we don't want to. Don't let this reason cause you to pray less.

Finally, we should pray because we really want to talk with God. **Read Psalm 63:1.** Have you ever been really thirsty? What do you think about at those times? *(Getting water.)* That should be your attitude about talking to God. We should desire at all times to talk to Him. **Scoop baking soda from the cup labeled "to desire to talk to God and praise Him" into the sixth balloon. Place the balloon over the sixth bottle and shake the baking soda into the vinegar. There will be a reaction.** God really loves it when we want to talk to Him. These kinds of prayers can accomplish much and cause amazing things to happen.

These are only some of the purposes of prayer. The most important thing to remember is to always have the right attitude when it comes to prayer.

APPLICATION: Circles of Prayer

 Before Class: Blow up a balloon. With masking tape, mark off a "start" and "finish" point at each end of the room.

Let's do a quick activity that will help us apply what we've learned about prayer.

Have students stand inside the lines in random order, wherever they wish. Hand the balloon to the person closest to the "start" point. When I say "go," pass your balloon from one person to another until the balloon reaches the finish line. Each person must pass the balloon at least one time. Let's see how fast we can pass it.

Say "go" and time the class to see how long it takes to get the balloon past the finish line. Make sure every person has had a chance to pass the balloon. The students will pass the balloon in a disorderly fashion because they have not had time to organize themselves.

I think we can do a better job of passing this balloon. This time, let's get organized. I'm going to assign some people certain jobs. **Select one person to begin the relay at the "start" line. Select another person to stand at the "finish" line. Select a third person to watch to make sure everyone gets a chance to pass the balloon. Then have students form a line from start to finish so that the balloon can be passed quickly. Say "go" and time your students.**

- Why were you able to pass the balloon more quickly the second time than the first time? *(We were more organized. I knew who to pass the balloon to.)*

Let's think of some other times when having a certain order helps to get things done.

- How does it help to use a certain order when you do a group project at school? *(Then people know what their jobs are and can do them better. There's less noise and confusion.)*

- Why is it so important for team members to have certain positions in a baseball game? *(So the game can be played right. So that people can do their parts to win the game.)*

There is also an order in prayer. When a Christian prays, God the Father, God the Son, and God the Holy Spirit all play different roles. Remember, we learned that God is three Persons in one. Each Person of the Trinity does something special to make sure your prayers are answered. Let's see what each Person in the Trinity does.

Read Matthew 6:6. God the Father is the One who hears and answers our prayers. **Write "Pray to God the Father" on the board. Read John 16:23.**

- What will happen when we pray to God the Father? *(He will reward us. He will give us what we ask.)*

Read John 14:12–14.

- In whose name do we pray? *(The name of Jesus.)*

Write "Pray in the name of Jesus" on the board.

This story will help us understand what it means to pray in the name of Jesus. One day, a young college student was invited by an older friend to go with him to visit Washington, D.C., our nation's capital. The college student was just expecting to see the sights, but something exciting happened. When they arrived, his friend took him to the White House where our country's president lives. There, the two of them spent the day as guests of the president and his wife. It turned out that the friend had known the president for years.

- What would have happened if the college student had tried to visit the president on his own? (*He would have been turned away. The President is too busy to see everyone who comes to Washington, D.C.*)

- What difference did it make that the college student went to the White House with someone who had been a friend of the president for years? (*The college student was welcomed into the White House. The college student could go places he couldn't go by himself.*)

- How is this story like using Jesus' name to talk to our heavenly Father in prayer? (*Jesus knows the Father so He helps us get His attention. Jesus can go to the Father any time because He is God's Son.*)

God honors those who pray in Jesus' name. When we do, God gives us a promise. **Read John 15:16.** God will give us what we ask for when we ask in Jesus' name. But using Jesus' name is not like chanting a magical phrase. We must believe that Jesus is the Son of God and obey Him to use His name.

But what does the Holy Spirit do in our prayers? **Read Romans 8:26,27. Write "The Holy Spirit helps our praying" on the board.** When we are filled with the Holy Spirit and we pray, the Holy Spirit helps us to pray like we should. He helps us to pray according to God's will. He also goes before God the Father and explains what our heart attitude is about our prayer. He is our Helper in prayer.

- Why do you think it is so important that the Holy Spirit helps us pray? (*Sometimes we don't know how to pray with the right words. He helps us to pray about the things God wants us to pray about. The Holy Spirit is God so He can explain what we need and want to the Father.*)

- Why do you think it is so important that all the three Persons in the Trinity are involved when Christians pray? (*The Persons of the Trinity always do important things together. God thinks praying is very important.*)

- What do you think sin in our lives does to our praying? (*It keeps us from praying because our hearts are not thinking about God. It keeps us from being filled with the Holy Spirit. God can't answer our prayers.*)

To review, we pray to God the Father because He answers our prayers. We pray in Jesus' name because God the Father listens to those who believe in His Son. And we pray the way we should with the help of the Holy Spirit who knows God's will.

Now, let's practice our praying. First, I want you to take a moment to think about any sin that may be cluttering up your life. Sin clogs the pipeline to God so that our prayers cannot reach God's ears. Practice Spiritual Breathing by confessing any sin you think of and then asking the Holy Spirit to fill you. **Give students time to reflect and pray.**

Hand out slips of paper and pencils. Divide students into groups of three and have each group form a prayer circle. In your prayer circle, you're going to pray for each other. Do this by having one person mention a prayer request. It could be about a problem that person is having, someone else who needs prayer, or a worry that he or she is thinking about. The other two people will write that student's name and request on their slips of paper. Then each of the other two people in your group will pray for that prayer request. When you finish, have the second person give a request, and so on. Be sure to pray to God the Father in Jesus' name.

Give students time to pray in their circles. When all three students in the groups have had a chance to give at least one request and have it prayed for, close in prayer, thanking God for the privilege of prayer. Remind your students to follow the proper order for prayer. From this point on, gently remind students to pray to God the Father and in Jesus' name whenever you have prayer times.

WEEKLY ASSIGNMENT: Prayer Balloons

Give each student a balloon and have students blow them up and tie them. Then have them tape the prayer requests they wrote in their prayer circle on their balloons.

Use your prayer balloons to remember the friends in your prayer circle all week. You can pray for both the requests on the slip of paper and other things you can think of for the two people in your group. Tape your balloon in your bedroom so you can remember to pray every day. **Have students set their balloons aside until after class.**

 Teaching Tip: You may want to have the balloons blown up ahead of time to eliminate confusion.

CHECK FOR UNDERSTANDING: Pop the Question

Before Class: Write the following questions onto slips of paper. Roll the slips and insert each one into a balloon. Inflate the balloons and tie them closed. Do not include the answers to the questions; they are for your information only.

- Who do we pray to? *(God the Father.)*
- Whose name do we use to pray? *(Jesus' name.)*
- Who helps us pray like we should? *(The Holy Spirit.)*
- What can keep God from hearing our prayers? *(If we have unconfessed sin.)*
- What are some good purposes for prayer? *(To glorify God; to ask God to supply what we need; to desire to talk to God and praise Him.)*
- What are some wrong purposes for prayer? *(To selfishly ask for things we want but do not need; to look good or impress others; because others want us to pray but we don't want to.)*

Allow a volunteer to select a balloon, pop it by sitting or stepping on it, and read the question. Have a second volunteer answer the question. Do this until all balloons are popped.

MEMORY VERSE ACTIVITY: Balloon Bust

1. 1 John 5:14,15

2. This is the confidence we have in approaching God:

3. that if we ask anything according to his will, he hears us.

4. And if we know that he hears us

5. —whatever we ask—

6. we know that we have what we asked of him.

Before Class: Write the numbers 1 to 6 on six slips of paper. Make two sets. Blow up two sets of six balloons, using a different color for each set. Place a slip of numbered paper in each balloon before tying it shut. Keep the sets separate.

Write the memory verse on the board and number each part as shown. Read it to the class.

As we've discussed in this lesson, we can be very confident in approaching God if our purpose is right and if we know Jesus as our personal Savior. **Read the memory verse together.** That's what this verse is saying. **Read the verse together a couple more times.** Let's play a balloon game to memorize the verse.

You will notice that I have numbered each part of the verse. Inside each of these balloons is a number. We will pop each balloon one at a time and erase the part with that number. Then we will say the whole verse. We will do this until all balloons are popped and the verse is completely erased. **Have different students come up one at a time and pop one of the balloons with a pin, then erase the part of the verse with the corresponding number. Continue until all parts are erased.**

Then take the other six balloons and use the same procedure in reverse, this time having students write each missing verse part on the board until the verse is complete.

Make sure each person has his or her prayer balloon and remind students to pray during the week. Close in prayer, thanking God for hearing and answering prayer.

All Shook Up

Plan for Prayer

LESSON PLAN

OBJECTIVE: Students will learn how to apply a simple guide to a daily prayer time.

APPLICATION: Students will begin using the ACTS method of prayer.

LESSON PLAN ELEMENT	ACTIVITY	TIME	SUPPLIES
Opening Activity	*A Prayer Pole*	9–10	A long wooden pole such as a broom or mop stick; 1 copy of "A Prayer Pole" handout; tape; scissors; push bell (optional)
Bible Story—Luke 11:1–4, Jesus teaches the disciples how to pray	*Lesson on Prayer*	5–10	4 large pieces of colored paper; scissors; tape; Bibles
Lesson Activity	*Using ACTS*	12–15	Bibles
Check for Understanding	*Toss-and-Tell Towel*	3–5	Towel; dry-erase marker or chalk
Application	*Prayer Pulls*	5–10	Jar, basket, or box; 1 copy of the "Missing Prayer Parts" handout; scissors
Memory Verse Activity	*Circling Around*	3–5	Dry-erase marker or chalk
Weekly Assignment	*ACTS Now*	3–5	Paper; markers

Effective prayer cannot be reduced to a magic formula. God does not respond to our requests because we have the right ritual. He is more interested in our hearts than our words. John Bunyan, author of *Pilgrim's Progress*, said, "In prayer it is better to have a heart without words than words without a heart."

God's Word does, however, give us certain basic elements that, when included in our communication with God, will enable us to receive His answers to our prayers. Those basic elements are adoration, confession, thanksgiving, and supplication—which spell out the acronym ACTS.

A—Adoration: To adore God is to worship and praise Him, to honor and exalt Him in our heart and mind and with our lips. God desires the fellowship of His children, of which adoration is a part (John 4:23,24; Hebrews 12:28). Adoration expresses our complete trust in Him and reflects our confidence that He hears us. Adoration demonstrates our reverence, awe, love, and gratitude.

C—Confession: When our discipline of prayer begins with adoration, the Holy Spirit has an opportunity to reveal any sin in our life that needs to be confessed. By seeing God in His purity, His holiness, and His love, we become aware of our sinfulness and unworthiness. Confessing our sin and receiving His forgiveness restores us to fellowship with Him and clears the channel for God to hear and answer our prayers (1 John 1:7–9).

T—Thanksgiving: Nothing pleases God more than our consistent expression of faith. What better way to do this than to tell Him, "Thank You"? God's Word commands us to give thanks (1 Thessalonians 5:18). An attitude of thanksgiving enables us to recognize that God controls all things—not just the blessings, but the problems and adversities as well. As we approach God with a thankful heart, He becomes strong on our behalf; conversely, a critical, unbelieving spirit displeases God and hinders His efforts to bless us and enrich us and to use us for His glory.

S—Supplication: Supplication includes petition for our own needs and intercession for others. We are to pray for everything in specific terms. For example, as you talk to God, pray that your inner person may be renewed, always sensitive to and empowered by the Holy Spirit. Pray about your problems, for wisdom and guidance, for strength to resist temptation, for comfort in time of sorrow—pray for everything (Philippians 4:6). Then pray for others—friends, parents, neighbors, your pastor, and missionaries. Pray for those in authority over you (1 Timothy 2:1,2). Pray especially that nonbelievers will receive Christ as their Savior and for opportunities to tell others about Jesus.

These elements will help your students develop a more well-rounded prayer life. The acronym will help them recall what to do when they pray.

LESSON PLAN

OPENING ACTIVITY: A Prayer Pole

Before Class: Cut apart the questions on "The Prayer Pole" handout. Number each question on the back of the paper. Tape one end of each question to the pole with the words facing you and the question numbers facing the students.

The answers to the questions are:

1. Who do we pray to? *(God, our heavenly Father.)*

2. What is God's delight? *(Our prayers.)*

3. What is one reason we should pray? *(To glorify God; to ask God to supply what we need; to desire to talk to God and praise Him.)*

4. What is one reason we should pray? *(To glorify God; to ask God to supply what we need; to desire to talk to God and praise Him.)*

5. What is one wrong purpose for prayer? *(To selfishly ask for things we want but do not need; to look good or impress others; because others want us to pray but we don't want to.)*

6. What is one wrong purpose for prayer? *(To selfishly ask for things we want but do not need; to look good or impress others; because others want us to pray but we don't want to.)*

7. In whose name should we pray? *(Jesus' name.)*

8. What stops God from hearing a Christian's prayers? *(Sin.)*

9. Who helps us pray? *(The Holy Spirit.)*

10. What should you do when you know there is sin in your life? *(Confess it.)*

11. How often should we give thanks to God? *(Always or continually.)*

12. What is the most powerful thing a Christian can do? *(Pray.)*

13. Who are the three Persons in the Trinity? *(God the Father; Jesus, God the Son; God the Holy Spirit.)*

14. What is Spiritual Breathing? *(Breathing out by confessing sin and breathing in by asking the Holy Spirit to fill me.)*

Note that questions 3 and 5 are repeated to allow students to give more than one answer.

To begin, ask students if they remembered to pray for their prayer-circle friends since the last lesson. Ask volunteers how God answered the requests they shared in their circles.

Ask for a volunteer to be the scorekeeper, then divide the remaining students into two groups. Last week we started talking about prayer.

* What is prayer? *(Talking to God.)*

Let's play a game called "Prayer Pole" to see how much we know about prayer.

Set the bell on a table in front of you. Ask one student from each team to come forward and stand near the bell. Have one of the students call out a question number for you to read. I am going to read this question. When you know the answer, ring the bell. Then give the answer out loud.

Read the question and give students time to ring the bell. If neither student knows the answer, allow students to confer with their teammates. The student who rings the bell first gets to answer first. Give a point to the team that answers correctly. Have those students return to their seats and a new student from each team come forward. The student from the team that won the previous point gets to choose the next question. Follow this procedure until all questions have been asked.

Congratulate the team with the most points, then say: For some of us, these questions were hard. Most of us don't know how to pray correctly. Jesus knew that about people too. While He was here on earth, Jesus taught His followers how to pray. Let's hear a Bible story about what He said to them.

BIBLE STORY: Lesson on Prayer

 Before Class: From the four large pieces of paper, cut out the letters "A," "C," "T," and "S."

Set out the letters you cut out and the tape. We can read about what Jesus taught His disciples in the Book of Luke.

Read Luke 11:1–4. As you can see, Jesus wanted to talk to His heavenly Father. To show how important prayer is, Jesus and His disciples went to a private place. He didn't want the crowds interrupting or distracting them.

The disciples must have been watching Jesus pray. They asked Him to teach them to pray.

* What do you think was different about Jesus' praying that made the disciples want to learn how to pray like He did? *(He was talking to God like He knew Him, because He did. Jesus got answers to His prayer all the time.)*

* What would you have wanted to know about prayer if you had been there? *(How to talk to God. What Jesus was praying about.)*

Make sure students have Bibles and ask them to turn to Luke 11:2. The first part of the prayer Jesus taught His disciples goes like this: "Father, hallowed be your name." Notice that Jesus begins His prayer by talking to His heavenly Father. We learned about this in our last lesson. Our prayer should always be directed to God the Father.

When Jesus says, "Hallowed be your name, your kingdom come," He is saying, "May your name be honored." This is a way of praising God. Praise is another word for adoration, adoring God. This means telling God how wonderful He is and how much we love Him. **Have a volunteer tape the "A" on one wall.** That "A" stands for "adoration." Some ways of adoring God are telling Him how wonderfully He created the world, how marvelous He is for being eternal and all-powerful, and how much He has done.

Next, in verse 3, Jesus prays, "Give us each day our daily bread." This type of request, made to God the Father, is called "supplication." Supplication means praying for things we need, like clothing or food, or for other people, such as our parents, neighbors, teachers, and friends. It also means praying when we're in trouble and need God's help. **Have a volunteer tape the "S" on another wall.** Supplication is asking God for something.

Next, in verse 4, Jesus prays, "Forgive us our sins, for we also forgive everyone who sins against us. And lead us not into temptation." This part of prayer is called confession. **Have a volunteer tape the "C" on a third wall.** We have already talked about confession, which is admitting our sins to God and asking Him to forgive them. Notice that Jesus also teaches us to ask God to keep us from committing more sins.

There is one other part of prayer that the Bible talks about that Jesus didn't mention here. That is thanksgiving. **Have a volunteer tape the "T" on another wall.** We must give God thanks for all the good things He has given us and also for what seem like problems in our lives. We thank Him for answering our prayers. He wants us to thank Him for everything.

The first letters of adoration, confession, thanksgiving, and supplication spell the word ACTS. That is a good way to remember all four parts of prayer.

In our Lesson Activity, we'll learn more about how to pray by using the ACTS method.

LESSON ACTIVITY: Using ACTS

Make sure each student has a Bible. Pair the students. Now I'm going to give you some Bible verses to see if you can recognize which part of prayer each one describes: "A," "C," "T," or "S." **Have students call out the words for each letter to help them remember the categories.** With your partner, look up the verse, decide which type of prayer it is, and go stand under the letter that represents that word. Don't let other people make up your mind for you; make your own decisions. As long as you have a good reason for selecting that letter, it's right.

Give each of the following verse references one at a time. Give pairs time to read and stand beneath a letter. Assist students who have a hard time finding verses in their Bibles. Discuss how the verse fits the word. Give leeway to pairs who come up with good reasons for standing under a different letter.

Psalm 148:1,2 *(Adoration.)*

Psalm 95:1,2 *(Thanksgiving.)*

Isaiah 59:1,2 *(Confession.)*

Acts 12:5 *(Supplication.)*

2 Timothy 1:3 *(Thanksgiving.)*

Jeremiah 32:17 *(Adoration.)*

Psalm 102:1,2 *(Supplication.)*

Psalm 51:1,2 *(Confession.)*

When you finish, gather students around you and ask the following questions.

- Which part of prayer do you most often forget to do? *(Adoration, because I didn't know what it meant. Thanksgiving, because I get busy and forget.)*

- Which part of prayer do you most often remember to do? *(Supplication, because I ask God for lots of things. Thanksgiving because I like to thank God.)*

- Which part of prayer do you think is the hardest to do? *(Confession, because I always forget to say sorry to God when I do something wrong. Adoration, because it's hard to think of something to say.)*

Of course, we don't have to use each part of prayer each time we pray. Sometimes, you might just need to quickly ask God for help or to confess a sin you just committed. You may want to just praise God for something or thank Him quickly. But most of the time, we will want to include all the parts of ACTS. Let's check to see how much you learned about the four parts of prayer.

CHECK FOR UNDERSTANDING: Toss-and-Tell Towel

On the board, write the four words *Adoration, Confession, Thanksgiving,* and *Supplication.* Tie up the towel so that it is in the shape of a ball.

We have been learning the four parts of prayer today. I am going to throw this towel to you and say one of the parts of prayer. You must then give an example of that part of the prayer. For example, if I toss you the towel and say "Supplication," you would answer with a supplication such as "Please help me do well on the exam I studied for." Then you will toss the towel to a friend and name another part of prayer, and your friend will give an example of it. **Do this as many times as needed to ensure that your students understand the four parts of prayer.**

APPLICATION: Prayer Pulls

 Before Class: Cut apart the prayers on the "Missing Prayer Parts" handout and put them into the container.

We have been discussing the four parts of prayer that Jesus taught us to include in our own prayers. Let's read some prayers and see if you can figure out which part is missing.

Choose a student to come up and pull out a prayer. Have the student read the prayer

aloud, then choose someone to tell which part of the prayer is missing. Do this with all four prayers. If possible, have the students insert a sentence for the part that is missing. When finished, review the four parts of prayer once again.

 Teaching Tip: If your students have a low reading ability, let the students choose a prayer for you to read.

These are the answers to the missing parts of the prayers:

Prayer 1: *(Confession missing.)*

Prayer 2: *(Adoration missing.)*

Prayer 3: *(Supplication missing.)*

Prayer 4: *(Thanksgiving missing.)*

MEMORY VERSE ACTIVITY: Circling Around

1 Thessalonians 5:17,18—"Pray continually; give thanks in all circumstances, for this is God's will for you in Christ Jesus."

Write the verse on the board. Then have students sit in a circle. Today we learned how to pray. The Bible says in 1 Thessalonians 5:17,18: **Read verses.** It is not enough just to know how to pray; we must pray without stopping. Often we pray maybe once a day, or sometimes only once a week. But this verse tells us that we should be doing it all the time. Throughout the day, we should be talking to God like we would to our best friend.

Let's practice our verse today by saying it continually. Each one of you will say one word of the verse in order as we go around the circle. You can look at the board to help you. We will do this several times, then I will erase the words on the board. If you can't remember the next word, you will have to sit inside the circle until we start the verse again. **Do this as many times as necessary for the students to learn the verse. Close by saying it together.**

WEEKLY ASSIGNMENT: ACTS Now

Give each student a marker and a piece of paper. Have students fold their paper in half, then in half again to make a four-page book. Using markers, have them write an "A," "C," "T," or "S" on each page of their paper.

This week, take time to pray once a day using your ACTS book. Each time you pray, write down one thing for each part of ACTS. For example, you might write for "A," "You are so powerful"; for "C," a sin you need to confess, like getting angry; for "T," "the beauty of the stars last night" as a thank-you; and for "S," a request for God to help you be nicer to your best friend who made you angry today. Bring your booklet with you to our next session and be prepared to share about your prayers.

Close by praying for your class, using all parts of the ACTS prayer plan.

The Prayer Pole

Who do we pray to?

What is God's delight?

What is one reason we should pray?

What is one reason we should pray?

What is one wrong purpose for prayer?

What is one wrong purpose for prayer?

In whose name should we pray?

What stops God from hearing a Christian's prayers?

Who helps us pray?

What should you do when you know there is sin in your life?

How often should we give thanks to God?

What is the most powerful thing a Christian can do?

Who are the three Persons in the Trinity?

What is Spiritual Breathing?

Missing Prayer Parts

Prayer 1

Dear Heavenly Father:

You are so creative! Your world that You created is a masterpiece. You are a Master Creator. Thank You for the beauty I see every day. Help me to care for your masterful work by helping Mom weed the garden. Help me to do this with a good attitude.

In Jesus' name,

Amen

Prayer 2

Dear Heavenly Father:

I confess I told a lie today. Please forgive me. Thank You for Your forgiveness and love. Please help me to do the right thing by helping me to tell the truth in the future.

In Jesus' name,

Amen

Prayer 3

Dear Heavenly Father,

You are such a wonderful, loving God. You knew me and loved me even before I was born. I confess I don't show love to my brother at times. Forgive me for calling him names. Thank You for never doing things like that to me. Thank You for showing me love always.

In Jesus' name,

Amen

Prayer 4

Dear Heavenly Father:

Oh, God, You are a majestic and powerful God. Your greatness awes me. I confess that I often forget about You and think only of myself. Help me to be less selfish. Help me to think more about You every day.

In Jesus' name,

Amen

LESSON 11

Power in Prayer

LESSON PLAN

Objective: Students will learn how to claim by faith the great power available through prevailing prayer.

Application: Students will plan ways to prevail in prayer through a daily prayer plan.

LESSON PLAN ELEMENT	ACTIVITY	TIME	SUPPLIES
Opening Activity	*Keeping Sharp*	7–10	Electric pencil sharpener; cloth; unsharpened pencils (one for each student plus one for the teacher; #2 soccer pencils would add a special touch); 3 metal fingernail files; 4 sheets of paper
Bible Story—Acts 12:1–19, Peter's miraculous escape from jail	*The Miracle of Prayer*	10–15	Bible; slips of paper; pencils
Lesson Activity	*Skill Strengthening*	8–10	Soccer ball; soccer poster (optional); "Prayer Skills" handout; pencils
Check for Understanding	*Prayer Skills*	3–5	"Prayer Skills" handouts; pencils
Application	*Gutting It Out*	5–10	Bible
Memory Verse Activity	*Pass Along*	5–7	Soccer ball; dry-erase marker or chalk
Weekly Assignment	*Prayer "Scorecards"*	2–3	"Prayer Scorecard" handouts; pencils

Missionary Jonathan Goforth was a man of powerful prayer. It is said that once he felt assured of God's will in prayer, he would continue in prayer until the thing was accomplished.

Andrew Murray, too, was a great prayer warrior. He wrote in *Praying Christian:* "The Christian needs strength. This we all know. The Christian has no strength of his own. This is also true."

Where may strength be obtained? Notice the answer: "Be strong in the Lord and in His mighty power" (Ephesians 6:10).

Paul spoke of this power earlier in his epistle to the Ephesians (1:18–20). He had prayed to God to give the Ephesian Christians the Spirit that they might know the greatness of His power—the mighty power He exerted in Christ when He raised Him from the dead.

This is the literal truth: The greatness of His power, which raised Christ from the dead, works in every believer. In me and in you. We hardly believe it, and still less do we experience it. That is why Paul prays, and we must pray with him, that God, through His Spirit, will teach us to believe in His almighty power.

Pray with all your heart: "Father, grant me the Spirit of wisdom, that I may experience this power in my life."

Pray for God's Spirit to enlighten your eyes. Believe in the divine power working within you.

Pray that the Holy Spirit may reveal it to you, and appropriate the promise that God will manifest His power in your heart, supplying all your needs.

Do you not begin to realize that time is needed—much time in fellowship with the Father and the Son, if you would experience the power of God within you? Your students need to understand this truth also. Their immaturity will hinder them from persevering in prayer, but sometimes their faith in God's ability and promise to answer may be greater than that of adults'.

How then can we help them extend their faith into perseverance? By relating their praying to an area familiar to them. One area in which preteens do display more perseverance is in sports. Use this quality to help them understand the importance of prevailing prayer. Help them use their developed sports endurance to prevail in prayer.

LESSON PLAN

OPENING ACTIVITY: Keeping Sharp

 Before Class: Set the electric pencil sharpener on a table at the front of the class. Cover it with the cloth so it can't be seen. Set out four pencils and three files.

Encourage students to share their prayer experiences from their ACTS prayer booklets. Compliment your students for their efforts in prayer.

Today, we are going to start our lesson by having a pencil-sharpening race. I need three volunteers to be in this race. **Choose three students. Have them come up and stand by the table. Give each a pencil and a nail file. Set out four pieces of paper.**

We are going to race to see who can get their pencil sharpened the fastest by using these metal files. When you have your pencil sharpened well enough, write your name on the paper in front of you. I will be racing against you too.

Tell the students to begin, then slowly reveal the electric pencil sharpener and sharpen your pencil. Write on your paper, "Prayer is our power source!" and your name. Hold it up, then read it aloud. Let the students finish sharpening if they choose. Most students will say something like, "That's not fair!" This will fit right into what you are trying to accomplish.

As you pointed out, this race wasn't quite fair. I used an electric sharpener while the others had to use a dull file. But did you know that we do something like this in our Christian walk? We have a great power source—Jesus. We can connect to Him through prayer anytime. But often we try to do everything on our own without the help of Jesus. We are not connected to the power source because we don't pray. We don't "plug in" to God's power through prayer.

Let's listen to a story about a man who was connected to the source and the miraculous event that occurred as a result.

Have students come up and get a pencil to sharpen. Have them use the pencil for the remaining activities in the lesson.

BIBLE STORY: The Miracle of Prayer

Distribute a slip of paper to each student. Point out Acts 12:1–19. Then tell the following Bible story.

This Bible story is pretty amazing. I want you to listen carefully. When I come to a certain point in the story, I'll ask a question and give you three options from which to choose. Write the option number you choose on your paper. When you find out the right answer, check off your answer if it was wrong.

Herod, the ruler of Palestine, hated Christians. He didn't want them to preach the good news about Jesus to anyone. He hated them so badly that he did something terrible. He arrested some of the Christians, intending to persecute them. One of these Christians was James, the brother of John. Herod ordered his soldiers to put John to death with a sword. When he did this, he noticed that many people in the city of Jerusalem were pleased. It made them happy that one of the Christians had died.

Peter knew all that was happening. James was his friend. I'm sure Peter was sad that James had been killed. But he also knew that now James was with Jesus in heaven. What do you think Peter did?

1. Stop preaching about Jesus to avoid being killed.

2. Only tell the people he trusted about Jesus.

3. Keep preaching in spite of the danger to his own life.

Give students time to write down a number.

The right answer is number 3. Peter kept on preaching. Nothing anyone could do to him would keep him from telling others about Jesus. And more and more people became Christians as a result. The church was growing!

Herod's soldiers then arrested Peter and put him in jail. Herod wanted to make sure that Peter didn't escape from jail, so he ordered Peter to be guarded by four squads of soldiers with four soldiers in each squad. In other words, Peter had sixteen soldiers guarding just him. Herod planned to put Peter on trial in a few days after the Passover celebration.

What do you think the church members in Jerusalem did?

1. Moved to another city, making sure they weren't going to get arrested too.

2. Told everyone they had no idea who Peter was.

3. Prayed for Peter.

Give students time to write down a number.

The right answer is number 3. The people in the church gathered to pray for Peter. The people were very afraid for his life. But they knew that God had power, so they gathered in one house and prayed. Although they prayed earnestly, nothing seemed to happen. Days went by, but Peter was still in jail in danger for his life. It looked hopeless.

Finally, the day before the trial came. Peter was still in jail. The sun went down. Peter fell asleep between the two soldiers who were chained to him. Sentries stood at the entrance of the prison. Herod was making sure that no one got in or out.

If you were Peter, what would you be thinking?

1. God is in charge even if it doesn't look like it.

2. I'm doomed, and tomorrow I'll probably die.

3. All my friends have deserted me.

Give students time to write.

Since Peter was sleeping, I suspect he wasn't worried. A good answer would be number 1. No matter what happened to him, he knew that God would be with him—whether he lived or died.

Then something strange happened. While he was sleeping, an angel appeared in the prison. A light brightened up the cell Peter was in. The angel poked Peter on the side and said, "Quick, get up!" The chains fell off Peter's wrists.

The angel said, "Put on your clothes and sandals." Peter did what the angel said. "Wrap your cloak around you and follow me." Peter followed the angel out of the prison.

What do you think Peter was thinking?

1. Wow! God sent an angel to save me!

2. I must be having a dream. This can't be happening.

3. What if someone sees what's happening? I might be in even more trouble.

Give students time to write.

The right answer is number 2. Peter was stunned; he thought he was having a dream.

The angel led him past the first group of guards. Nothing happened. Then they went past the second group of guards. Nothing happened. Then they came to the iron gate leading to the city. The gate opened by itself, and Peter and the angel went through it. Then as they were walking down the street, the angel disappeared. Peter was left alone.

At that point, what do you think Peter was thinking?

1. Hey, I made it out alive!

2. Maybe I'd better go back to the prison before the guards discover that I'm missing.

3. The Lord sent an angel and rescued me from Herod's clutches!

Give students time to write.

The right answer is number 3. Finally, Peter realized that God was in charge and that God had sent the angel to rescue him. So Peter went right to the house of Mary, the mother of John Mark, where the people had been praying all night for him. Peter knocked on the door and a young girl named Rhoda answered the door. She peeked out to see who it was before she unlocked it.

How do you think Rhoda reacted when she saw Peter?

1. She got so excited that she forgot to open the door.

2. She said, "Go away, Peter. We don't want you around anymore! You get into too much trouble."

3. She was overjoyed to see Peter.

Give student time to write.

Rhoda was so overjoyed to see Peter that she forgot to open the door. The right answer is number 1. She ran back to where the others were praying, shouting, "Peter is at the door!"

What do you think those who were praying said?

1. "God rescued Peter!"

2. "Rhoda, you're out of your mind!"

3. "I really don't want Peter in here because he might bring soldiers here too."

Give students time to write.

Actually, the people said number 2, "Rhoda, you're out of your mind!" Although they were praying, they didn't believe God would answer. They had prayed so long with nothing happening that their faith had gotten dim. They said, "It must be Peter's angel."

Peter just kept on knocking. When they opened the door, they were so surprised to see him. Then Peter told them all about the miraculous thing the Lord had done by sending an angel.

But what happened to the guards? In the morning when they awoke, they found Peter missing. "Where is he?" they asked, mystified. They searched everyone in the prison but they couldn't find him.

When Herod heard about what had happened, he cross-examined each guard. But they could tell him nothing.

Have volunteers tell how they did on their answers.

- What was God's answers to the Christians' prayers? (*He sent an angel to get Peter out of prison. He saved Peter's life.*)

- Why do you think God waited so long to answer their prayers? (*Perhaps so their faith would get stronger when they saw what God had done. Maybe so that everyone knew for sure that God answers prayer. It didn't seem like a long time to God.*)

- How did the people respond to God's answer to prayer? (*At first, they couldn't believe Peter was there. Then they were joyful.*)

- How do you think this whole situation changed the people's ideas about prayer? (*They had more faith that God would answer. They prayed for even more things than before.*)

- How do you feel when you pray about a situation that seems hopeless? (*I really believe God will answer my prayer. I don't have any hope of anything good happening even though I've prayed.*)

- How does seeing God answer your prayers in a powerful way change your feelings about prayer? (*I pray more. I'm more thankful to God. I understand better how powerful God is.*)

In our Lesson Activity, we'll find out more about what God thinks of our praying.

LESSON ACTIVITY: Skill Strengthening

 Before Class: Hang up your soccer poster if you brought one.

Distribute the "Prayer Skills" handout. Make sure all students have Bibles. Hold up the soccer ball.

* What sport uses this ball? *(Soccer.)*

* When you play soccer, do you become a great player overnight? Why or why not? *(No, because you have to practice. Great players have to start at the beginning and learn all the rules and all the skills of soccer.)*

* What are some things you need to know to become a great player? *(How to kick, pass, receive. How to move the ball up and down the field.)*

On your "Prayer Skills" handout, notice the drawing of the soccer player. Look at his head first. In soccer, more than most other sports, a player uses his head to move the ball. Beside the player's head, write *head skills.* **Demonstrate this or have a student demonstrate this skill with the soccer ball.**

Now look at the player's chest and thigh. These are areas where a soccer player must learn to receive a ball. Write *receiving skills* here. **Demonstrate this or have a student demonstrate this skill.**

Look at the soccer player's feet. He uses them to dribble and pass the ball. Write *dribbling and passing skills* here. A great soccer player must work on these skills and practice them daily. **Demonstrate this or have a student demonstrate this skill.**

Just like a soccer player, did you know that a Christian should have qualities and conditions that they practice daily to pray with power? Let's look at what the Bible says about this. Look at the picture of the person praying on your handout. Find Hebrews 11:1,6 in your Bible. **Have a volunteer read the verse aloud.**

* What is one quality that we need? *(Faith in God.)*

Write that by the head of the praying person. **Have a volunteer read Romans 12:1,2.**

* What does this verse say we need to do? *(Yield to God.)*

Write this by the hands. **Have a volunteer read Mark 11:25.**

* What should our attitude be? *(Forgiving.)*

Write this by the heart. **Have a volunteer read 1 John 3:22.**

* What does this verse say we need to do to have powerful prayers? *(Obey God's commands.)*

Write "obey God" by the feet.

Just as a soccer player must work daily on game skills, so a Christian must practice faith, yield to God, forgive others, and obey God's commands daily. If we allow sin in our life or a lack of faith, our prayers will not be powerful.

A soccer player cannot score a goal unless conditions are right. He or she has to count on teammates to help make it possible. A Christian also has conditions that are in place for an answer to prayer. **Read 1 John 5:14,15.** God will not answer any prayer that goes against what is best for us. Write "Pray according to God's will" somewhere on your handout.

Read Matthew 18:19. We can also increase our power in prayer by praying with other Christians. Just as a soccer player can't play the game as well without his or her teammates, we can have more power in prayer by praying with others. Write "Pray with others" somewhere on your handout.

CHECK FOR UNDERSTANDING: Prayer Skills

Have students turn their handouts over so they can't see them. Then see if they can remember what they wrote beside each part of the body. Have them write the necessary action on the back of their handout as you name the part of the body:

Head—*(faith in God)*

Hands—*(yield to God)*

Heart—*(forgive others)*

Feet—*(obey God)*

Then see if they can remember the other statements they wrote on their papers:

("Pray according to God's will.")

("Pray with others.")

Have students turn over their papers and check their answers. Compliment students who got the answers right.

APPLICATION: Gutting It Out

 Before Class: Think of an example to share with the class of prevailing prayer, in which you or someone else prayed for a long time and eventually saw the answer.

Let's do some exercises that a soccer player might do to help get ready for a game.

Have students do some of the following exercises:

- **Running in place**
- **Jumping rope**
- **Jumping jacks**

- **Push ups**

- **Sit ups**

Keep doing these exercises long enough so that some members of the group stop or slow down.

- Was it hard to keep going when you got tired? Why? *(Yes, because I didn't have any energy left. Yes, I just couldn't keep doing them because my muscles wore out.)*

- Can you think of other times when you found it hard to keep going? *(Doing laps in Physical Education class; taking long hikes; making bike trips; raking a big yard.)*

When soccer players are involved in a long, tough game, it is often hard for them to keep going. But they reach deep inside for some extra strength. This is sometimes called "gutting it out." We can compare this to our prayer life. We often find that not every prayer is answered right away. Often we have to pray for weeks, months, and even years before our prayer is answered. We call this "prevailing prayer." Jesus talked about this in Luke 18:1–8. **Read this passage to your students.**

- From hearing this story, how long does God think we should pray about something? *(God wants us to keep praying a long time. He doesn't want us to give up when we don't get an answer right away.)*

- What does God promise will happen if we keep praying? *(He will give us justice. He will make sure things work out right.)*

One thing to remember: Prayers need to be in line with God's will. If you pray against God's will, God will not answer. For example, if you pray that someone who was mean to you will get hit by a car, God won't listen to that prayer. He wants us to love everyone, even those who treat us badly. So we must make sure our prayers go along with God's commands in His Word.

Just like the widow in the story, we are to be persistent in coming to God about things we need. If He doesn't answer right away, we should "gut it out" and keep asking. Think about a prayer request that you have been asking God about for a while. **Share your example of prevailing prayer.**

- Do you have an example of prevailing prayer in your life or someone else's life that you'd like to share? *(Allow volunteers to share. When they do, point out why God may have waited to answer or what good things happened as a result.)*

This is called prevailing prayer. God wants us to not give up on asking Him for this request. He wants us to be persistent. Let's take a moment right now and pray for the requests that you have been prevailing in pray about.

Take a moment for silent prayer.

MEMORY VERSE ACTIVITY: Pass Along

James 5:16—"The prayer of a righteous man is powerful and effective."

Write the verse on the chalkboard or white board. Read the verse aloud.

Do you see the qualification in this verse? Not everyone can pray and get answers to his prayers. The person praying must be righteous. Only those who have received Jesus as their Savior are righteous. We are righteous because our sins have been forgiven by the blood of Jesus.

To be righteous, we must also keep our sins confessed. If our hearts are pure, free from our past sin, our prayers will be more effective. They will have more power. We will keep the pipeline open to God's prayer answers. We will then accomplish what God wants us to accomplish!

Have students stand in a line, about two feet apart. (You may want to do this activity outside or in a long hallway. If so, write the verse on poster board.) Start by placing the soccer ball at the feet of the first person in line. If some of your students have never played soccer and do not know how to pass the ball with their feet, have one student demonstrate before you begin.

Pass this ball to the person in front of you using only your feet. Do not kick; just pass or dribble with your feet. As you pass it, say one word of the memory verse. The reference counts as one word. The person you pass it to will say the next word, then pass the ball to the next person.

Keep passing the ball, going through the memory verse until your students know the verse. (When the ball reaches the last person in line, have students pass the ball in the reverse direction.) Then repeat the verse as a class. Ask volunteers to recite the verse from memory. All the students should be able to memorize this verse.

WEEKLY ASSIGNMENT: Prayer "Scorecards"

When you play many sports such as golf, bowling, and basketball, you usually keep a scorecard. A soccer coach will often keep a statistical scorecard. He or she will record not only when a player scores, but all the passes, dribbles, kicks, and assists. Sometimes, this information is reported in the newspaper.

We can keep a "scorecard" on our prayers. **Distribute the "Prayer Scorecard" handout.**

Keep track of your answered prayers and prevailing prayers. Look at the top set of columns. Earlier, you learned what prevailing prayer was. You prayed for a prevailing request. Write that request under the prevailing request column. Write today's date in the second column. Each time you pray for this request, write the date in the column. When the prayer is answered, write the answer and the date in the third column. During the week, write down any requests for which you have been praying and need to keep praying. Perhaps you have been praying for a family member to become a Christian.

Also record other individual prayer requests, such as for a test you have coming up soon.

Write these in the bottom set of columns. Do the same thing with these requests as for the prevailing requests. Each time you pray for these requests, write the date in the second column. When the prayer is answered, write the answer and the date in the third column.

Post your scorecard in your room. Continue to add new requests when these have been answered. Also post your "Prayer Skills" handout so that you can remember the skills to practice to have power in prayer. Next session, we will talk about what you prayed about and if you were able to keep praying without giving up. Bring your "Prayer Scorecards" with you to our next lesson.

Close in prayer, asking God to help your students persist in praying each day and for requests that aren't answered right away. During the week, keep your students' prayer practices before God's throne. Part way through the week, you may want to call your students to encourage them.

Prayer Skills

Prayer "Scorecard"

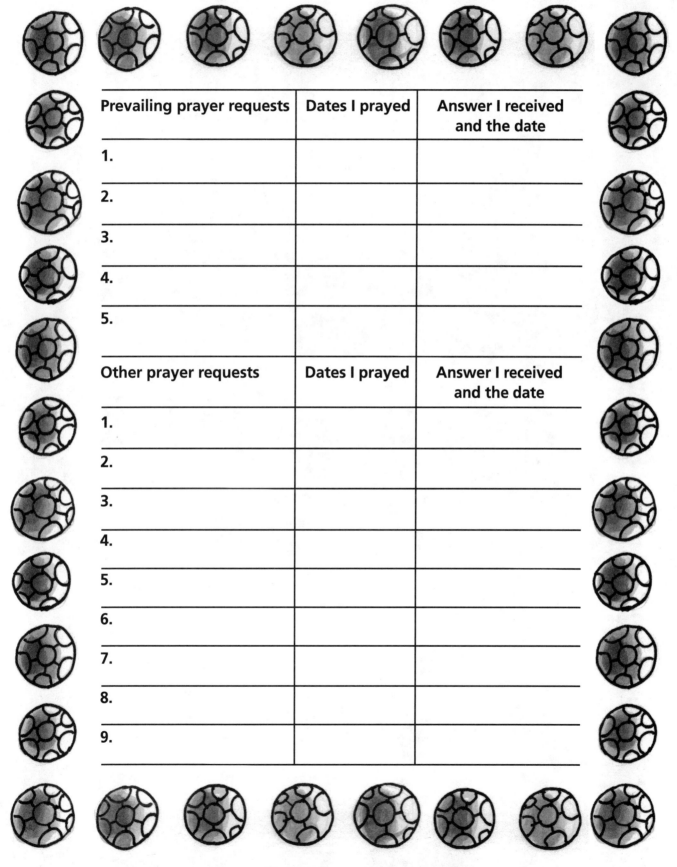

Prevailing prayer requests	Dates I prayed	Answer I received and the date
1.		
2.		
3.		
4.		
5.		
Other prayer requests	Dates I prayed	Answer I received and the date
1.		
2.		
3.		
4.		
5.		
6.		
7.		
8.		
9.		

LESSON 12

Promises for Prayer

LESSON PLAN

OBJECTIVE: Students will learn how to claim God's promises in prayer.

APPLICATION: Students will plan a definite place, time, and activities for spending time with God and for claiming promises from Scripture in their prayers.

LESSON PLAN ELEMENT	ACTIVITY	TIME	SUPPLIES
Opening Activity	*Wacky Water Temperature*	5–8	3 water buckets; cold water; tepid water; warm water; thermometer
Bible Story—John 13:31–14:14, Jesus is the way to heaven	*Road Map to Heaven*	12–15	Bible; 3 copies of "Cougar County Map" handouts; pencils; paper
Lesson Activity	*God Is Dependable*	7–10	Bibles; "Cougar County Map" handouts; pencils; 3" squares of paper; chalk or dry-erase marker; cellophane tape
Check for Understanding	*Map Check*	3–5	"Cougar County Map" handouts
Application	*Taking Time Out for God*	5–7	Bible; "My Time With God" handouts; pencils
Memory Verse Activity	*Surfing for Scripture*	5–10	One pail of water used in Lesson Activity; 20 pieces of Styrofoam (1" or larger, cut from Styrofoam cups); permanent marker; chalk or dry-erase marker
Weekly Assignment	*Taking Action*	3–5	"My Time with God" handout; pencils

I t is estimated that there are more than 5,000 personal promises in the Bible. However, these promises mean little or nothing to many Christians because they do not claim them by faith (Hebrews 4:2).

Faith is a word signifying action. For example, bags of cement sitting in a warehouse will never become concrete until they are mixed with sand, gravel, and water. Likewise, God's promises will never become concrete unless they are mixed with faith and action. You must make them yours by believing them and putting your faith to work.

One way we put God's promises to work is through prayer. Our prayers reveal much about our spiritual condition. Are we asking God for more than we are able to do in our own strength? Are our prayer requests selfish or unselfish? Are we consistently talking to God? What is the attitude we bring to prayer?

This lesson will teach your students some of God's conditions and promises concerning prayer and His provision for their needs. Your students are eager for action, to do something that makes a difference. Their personalities and habits are still forming. There is no better time than now to introduce them to the promises of prayer! When you do, you will set them on a road to spiritual success and intimacy with God that will last a lifetime.

LESSON PLAN

OPENING ACTIVITY: Wacky Water Temperature

Before Class: Bring three water buckets, and just before class fill one with warm water, one with cold, and one with tepid water. Place them on a table in the front of the room. Put the warm and cold pails side by side and the tepid on the outside.

Go over your students' "Prayer Scorecards" from the previous lesson. Note how God has answered prayer over the last week. Encourage your students to keep praying for the requests that haven't been answered.

- What does dependable mean? *(Something you can count on; something reliable; it will always be there.)*

Today we are going to see how dependable our sense of touch is. I am sure many of you have touched something very hot or very cold. We have an immediate reaction to these sensations. We often think our sense of touch is very dependable. We are going to do an activity that will show us that our sense of touch is not as reliable as we think.

Divide students into groups of three. Have each group send one person to the front of the class. Have the students place one hand in cold water and the other in warm water for one minute. If possible, time it for them. Then have them put both hands in the pail of tepid water. Tell them to observe what each hand senses the temperature is. Have them dry their hands and return to their seats, then ask them these questions:

- Did your sense of touch differ from hand to hand in the tepid water? *(Yes.)*

- How did the tepid water feel to your hand that was in the cold water? *(Nice and warm.)*

- How did the tepid water feel to your hand that was in the warm water? *(Cold.)*

Each hand felt the water temperature differently, yet the tepid water temperature was the same. Our sense of touch in this instance was not reliable. **Hold up the thermometer.** The only way to get a reliable reading of the water temperature would be to use this thermometer. It will always read correctly. It is reliable. **Measure the water temperature in all three buckets.**

We can compare the thermometer to God. He can always be counted on. He never changes.

We are going to learn in our Bible story today that God is very dependable.

BIBLE STORY: Road Map to Heaven

To begin our Bible story, we will pretend that we are going on a trip. But only one of us knows how to get there.

Divide your class into three groups. Assign one student in each group as the Tour Guide. Make sure these students have good verbal skills. Give each Tour Guide a "Cougar County Map" handout and a pencil.

Tour Guides, do not let the other people in your group look at your Cougar County map. You will study your map so that you can explain to your group how to get from Misery Mall to the Good Times Cabin. Name the landmarks such as forks in the road, creeks, and so forth, to help you explain your route. Use a pencil to mark the route if you need to. You will have to explain the route to your group members without letting them see your map. Let's see how well you can do this.

Send Tour Guides to a corner of your room. While Tour Guides are studying their maps, distribute paper and pencils to the rest of the students and explain what they are to do.

When your Tour Guide returns, he or she will explain how to get from Misery Mall to the Good Times Cabin. Write down notes or draw pictures to help you remember the route you hear. Later in the Bible story, I'll ask some of you to describe the route to the Good Times Cabin.

Have the Tour Guides join their groups. Give Tour Guides enough time to explain the route to their group members. Circulate, checking to make sure Tour Guides do not show their maps to others. This exercise will be hard for your students.

After a few minutes, reconvene as a class, having group members sit near each other. Open your Bible to John chapter 13 and tell the story.

The disciples had spent a lot of time with Jesus. They had experienced amazing things—miracles, teaching, even seeing the dead come to life. Most recently, they had seen a great crowd around Jerusalem hail Jesus as their King as Jesus rode into the city on a donkey. The people waved palm branches and threw their coats on the road for His donkey to walk over. It was a great time to be alive!

But then Jesus started saying things to the disciples that got them all upset. He told them that He was going to die. He explained that He was going away to heaven. Let me read to you what the disciples said. **Read John 13:36,37 and 14:5.**

Isn't it hard when someone tells you that he or she is going somewhere and that you will follow later, but you don't know the way? Let's see how our Tour Guides did in explaining the route from Misery Mall to the Good Times Cabin. **From each group, have a volunteer (other than the Tour Guide) explain the route. This will be almost impossible for your students.**

As you can see, it's difficult to find your way to a place you've never been before. How were the disciples to find their way to where Jesus was going? Jesus was going to show them the way. They didn't have to worry. Jesus also promises us that He will show us the way to heaven. He is our Perfect Tour Guide.

The disciples asked Jesus to help them, and He promised He would. Today, Jesus is not here in His body, so we can't ask Him things the way the disciples did. But we can talk to

Him anytime we want. Of course, we talk to Him in prayer.

Philip asked Jesus a question, too. Let me read about it. **Read John 14:8–14.**

Jesus told us how we can have our prayer answered. **Reread John 14:14.** We must ask in Jesus' name.

- What does Jesus promise will happen when we do that? *(He will do what we ask.)*

This is called having a "condition" and a "promise." The condition is what we must do first. The promise is what Jesus will do in return. The condition here is that we must ask in Jesus' name. The promise is that when we do, God will answer our prayer.

Someone has counted 5,000 promises in the Bible. We just learned about one that had to do with prayer. Let's read about three others.

Read each of the following verses aloud. Then have students name the condition and the promise.

Jeremiah 33:3 *(Condition: Call to God; Promise: He will answer and tell us great things.)*

Matthew 21:22 *(Condition: Believe; Promise: We will receive whatever we ask for.)*

1 John 5:14,15 *(Condition: Ask according to God's will; Promise: He hears us, and we have what we ask of Him.)*

Let's compare our fun exercise with the Cougar County Map with Jesus' promises about prayer.

- What was different between our Tour Guides and Jesus as a tour guide? *(Our Tour Guides couldn't explain the route very well so we might not get to the cabin. We might even get lost. Jesus will make sure we get to heaven.)*

- Why do you think God gave us so many promises in the Bible? *(He loves us so much. He likes to make promises and keep them.)*

- How does it make you feel to know that there are that many promises in the Bible? *(Like God really loves me; that God cares about my prayers.)*

There is one important thing about promises—you have to trust the person who makes them. In our Lesson Activity, we'll see why we can trust God to keep His promises.

Before you continue to the next activity, allow the students to see the Cougar County Map and see what the Tour Guides were describing to them.

LESSON ACTIVITY: God Is Dependable

Have students remain in the same groups. Make sure each group has a Bible, a scrap of paper, and a pencil. Assign one person in each group to be the reader. God promises to do certain things for us when we pray. In your group, read the verses I assign you and decide what God promises to do. You will report your answer back to the class.

Assign each group two passages as shown. Possible answers are included in italics.

GROUP 1:

Philippians 4:19 *(He meets all our needs.)*

Psalm 84:11 *(He won't keep anything good from us.)*

GROUP 2:

Proverbs 3:5,6 *(He will make our paths straight.)*

Psalm 32:8 *(He will teach us and watch over us.)*

GROUP 3:

Ephesians 1:3 *(He blesses us with spiritual blessings.)*

Philippians 4:13 *(Jesus gives us strength to do everything we should do.)*

Allow groups to read and discuss. Then allow students to report their findings to the class. These promises of God cover three areas. The Group 1 promises relate to material things like food, clothing, and home; Group 2, guidance to know what to do; and Group 3, spiritual needs like love from God, help from the Holy Spirit to do what's right, and peace in our hearts. **Write these three areas on the board as you explain them.**

Together, these three areas cover all of our life. God is involved in everything we do.

- Who is the most dependable person in your life and why? *(My mom because she's always there for me. My grandma because she has time to help me. My dad takes me so many places.)*

God is even more dependable than these people we've mentioned.

Give each person a "Cougar County Map," five squares of paper, and a pencil. Make cellophane tape available. As we find out each way God is dependable, write it on one slip of paper. Then tape it somewhere on your route to the Good Times Cabin. This can help remind us that we can always depend on God to help us find our way in life.

Read each verse and ask volunteers to describe what the verse says about God's reliability. Write each answer on the board. Give students time to write down each way God is reliable before you read the next reference.

Psalm 9:10 *(God will not forsake us.)*

Psalm 115:11 *(God is our help and our shield from evil.)*

Isaiah 26:4 *(He is our eternal Rock, so we can always trust Him.)*

Nahum 1:7 *(God is our protection in trouble.)*

2 Samuel 7:28 *(He is sovereign and His word is trustworthy.)*

- We all have situations where we need to rely on God. What situation can you think of in which you are glad God is dependable? *(Give an example from your own life and then let the students share their thoughts. If students are having trouble relating circumstances to God's promise of dependability, have students give difficult situations and discuss as a class at least one of the verses above.)*

- What one thing do you need to pray for and which promise can you apply to it? *(Give an example from your life, then have students give their thoughts.)*

God's promises are real. We can believe them, claim them, and live by them. Let's learn about a way to help us believe, claim, and live by God's promises.

CHECK FOR UNDERSTANDING: Map Check

Have students turn over their "Cougar County Map" handouts and see if they can name the five ways God is dependable that they wrote on their maps. You may have to do this more than one time to help the students remember them.

APPLICATION: Taking Time Out for God

Jesus Christ gave us an example of what we need to do to spend time with God. **Read Mark 1:35.** He chose a place where He could be alone. He made sure it was someplace where He would not be distracted. That is what you need to do also.

Distribute the "My Time With God" handouts and pencils. To make sure that you develop a daily habit of time alone with God, the first thing you need to do is establish a definite place to spend this time. Find a place that is quiet and private. Probably the most ideal place is somewhere at home or in your bedroom. If this is impossible, perhaps you might choose a corner of your school library or a secret hideout. Write this place on your chart in the blank beside the words "Definite Place." **Give students time to do this. You might want to walk around and give ideas or help.**

Let me read Mark 1:35 again. **Read the verse.**

- When did Jesus go and pray? *(Early in the morning.)*

- Why do you think Jesus chose this time? *(He wanted to talk to God at the beginning of His day. It was quietest.)*

This was probably the best time for Jesus to pray. When is your best time? For some of you it is in the morning, or after school, or before you get ready for bed at night. Others may have another time. Whenever you have the most time is a good choice. You should pick a time with God that is unhurried. Set the time aside each day and remember to think only about God. Write the time you have chosen on the chart in the blank beside the words "Definite Time." **Give students time to do this.**

The last component of time with God is having definite activities planned. You might want to include some or all of the following activities. The first two are vital. They are Bible study or reading and prayer. If you have time to do only two activities, these would be the ones to choose. You might also want to include personal worship. You could sing or read a psalm to praise God. You might include writing a poem or letter to God to worship His majesty. You might play an instrument or listen to a song to worship Him. You could also spend some time just being quiet and thinking of the greatness of God. You can add other ways to the list if you choose. Look at the list of activities on your handout. Check off the ones you will regularly include. Circle the ones you will do occasionally. **Give students time to do this.**

- What do you think will happen in your life if you do these things every day? *(I will get closer to God. I will get lots more prayers answered. I will remember to do what God says.)*

- What are some reasons why it may be hard to do this every day? *(I get too busy. I might forget. I'd rather play with my friends or do something else.)*

- What do you think might happen if you don't talk to God and read His Word every day? *(I'll forget to do what God says. I won't get answers to my prayers because I didn't pray. I might do more bad things.)*

MEMORY VERSE ACTIVITY: Surfing for Scripture

Jeremiah 33:3—"Call to me and I will answer you and tell you great and unsearchable things you do not know."

 Before Class: Write one word from the verse on each piece of Styrofoam. (Place the reference on one piece.) Put the Styrofoam pieces into a pail word-side down.

Write the Scripture verse on the board or a poster. Write beside it 20 blank lines to represent each word and Scripture reference from Jeremiah 33:3.

Divide the students into two groups. Have students read the verse together. We learned today that God is dependable. He can be relied on to answer our prayers and listen to us. In this verse, God is telling us that if we call on Him, we can depend on Him to not only answer us but to show us great things as well. Let's read the verse a couple more times together. **After doing that, erase the verse on the board or turn the poster over. Leave the blanks on the board.**

Now we are going to surf for our Scripture verse in this pail of water. We'll have one person from Team 1 come forward and select a piece of foam from the surf. When you have chosen a word, you need to write it in the proper blank on the board. If you are correct, your team gets one point. If incorrect, the word is put back into the pail and your team receives no point. Then we'll have a member of Team 2 come forward to choose a word.

Do this until all words are chosen and written correctly on the board. Have the students once again recite the verse. You can erase the words and do it again if time permits. You may also choose to have individuals say the verse to you.

DISCOVERING OUR AWESOME GOD

WEEKLY ASSIGNMENT: Taking Action

Now that you have decided on a definite place, time, and activities, you are ready to take action and spend time with God this week. Look at the bottom half of your handout. This is a chart for next week. Fill in the dates beside the words "Week of." **Help students put in the date, such as Feb. 7–13.**

Each day this week you need to go to your definite place at your definite time. Do your planned activities. Write in the Scripture verses you read in the row labeled "Scripture I read." Put in the total amount of time you spent doing these activities in the row "Time I spent." If something stands out that day, like a thought from the Bible, an answered prayer, or a personal worship experience, write it in the row "Highlights I found." Be prepared to share with us about your times with God when we get together next week.

Close in prayer, asking God to help your students be consistent in their prayer times and in filling out their charts.

Cougar County Map

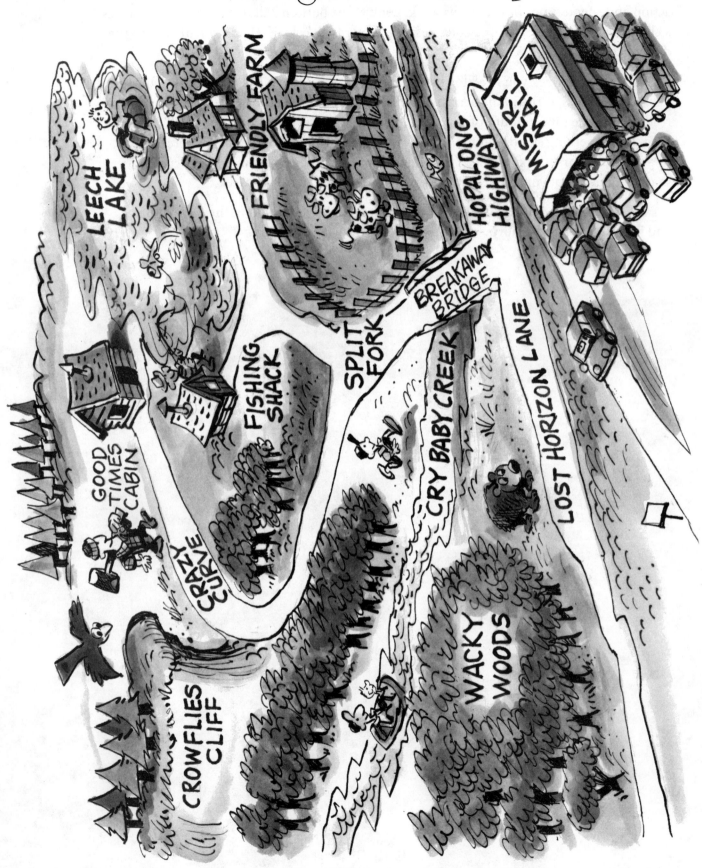

My Time With God

Definite Place _____

Definite Time _____

Activities I Choose

☐ Bible reading or Bible study

☐ Prayer

☐ Personal worship

    ☐ Sing a song

    ☐ Read a psalm of praise

    ☐ Write a poem or letter

    ☐ Play an instrument

    ☐ Listen to a worship song

    ☐ _____

☐ Quiet meditation

Week of _____

	Mon.	Tues.	Wed.	Thurs.	Fri.	Sat.
Scripture I read						
Time I spent						
Highlights I found						

Trinity Triangle

LESSON PLAN

OBJECTIVE: Students will learn how the members of the Trinity work together to accomplish God's work.

APPLICATION: Students will begin praying consistently to the Father, in the power of the Spirit, and in Jesus' name.

LESSON PLAN ELEMENT	ACTIVITY	TIME	SUPPLIES
Opening Activity	*The Trinity Twine*	7–10	Apple; knife; dry-erase marker or chalk; three 6" different-colored pieces of embroidery thread or yarn for each student (preferably red, white, and blue); masking tape	
Bible Story—assorted Scriptures, the Trinity	*Three in One*	10–15	1 copy of the "God Is" diagram from Lesson 1; 1 copy each of the four "Trinity Triangle" reproducibles; poster board; scissors; tape; Bibles	
Check for Understanding	*Tell It Again, Sam!*	3–5	Visuals from Bible story	
Lesson Activity	*Three Prayer Strands*	7–10	Bibles; chalk or dry-erase marker	
Application	*A Prayer With Three Strands*	7–10	Paper; pencils	
Memory Verse Activity	*Trinity Triangles*	3–5	Poster board; marker; scissors; sticky tack	
Weekly Assignment	*Using the Strands of Prayer*	3–5	Yarn braids from Opening Activity; paper clips	

Having a correct understanding of God changes us because our view of Him determines our lifestyle. What we believe to be true about God's character affects our friendships, work and leisure, the type of literature we read, and even the music we enjoy. Everything about our lives—our attitudes, motives, desires, actions, and even our words—are influenced by our view of God. This is just as true for your preteens.

The supreme purpose for humans is to know their God and Savior. Paul writes, "Everything else is worthless when compared with the priceless gain of knowing Christ Jesus my Lord. I have discarded everything else, counting it all as garbage, so that I may have Christ" (Philippians 3:8, NLT). We must get to know Him better.

Your students have gained a lot of information about God and His character. They have begun to implement this information into their lives. Of course, it will take much more encouragement and training for these young people to become spiritually mature. But they have taken foundational first steps.

This lesson puts together the concept of the Trinity for your students. Once again, they will be reminded that God works as one, even though He is three Persons. Emphasize the ongoing relationship with God that your students have developed. The Weekly Assignment will help them to continue in their prayer life. Also encourage them to faithfully read and study the Bible daily.

LESSON PLAN

DING! DONG!

OPENING ACTIVITY: The Trinity Twine

Discuss the "My Time With God" charts from the previous lesson and how consistently your students spent daily time with God. You may want to photocopy the handout again to distribute and encourage students to keep working on their devotion time.

Teaching Tip: Do not become discouraged if students are having difficulty keeping a consistent devotion time. Many adults struggle too. Also, don't give your students a sense of failure if they haven't been as consistent as you would like. Instead, encourage them to keep practicing like they would on a sport skill. What you have taught them about spending time with God will stay with them until they are older and can develop further discipline in this area.

On the chalkboard write the titles "skin," "flesh," and "core." Then show the students an apple.

- What words can we use to describe this apple? *(Shiny; red; delicious; hard; round.)*

Write the descriptive words on the board under the title "skin." Cut the apple in two and cut off a piece of the flesh.

- What words can we use to describe this part of the apple? *(White; soft; delicious; sweet; juicy.)*

Write the words on the board under the title "flesh." Take out the core and a seed. Show the students this part of the apple.

- What words can we use to describe the core? *(Black/brown; hard; inedible; small; seedy.)*

Write the words on the board under the title "core." Each of these parts—the skin, the flesh, and the core—are different, yet they all make up the apple.

Read 2 Corinthians 13:14. We have been learning about the three Persons of God—God the Father, God the Son, and God the Holy Spirit. They have three different personalities yet they are one God. It's like the apple. The parts are different, yet it's all one apple. It is the same with God.

The Bible talks about a cord with three strands. It says in Ecclesiastes 4:12, "A cord of three strands is not quickly broken." Let's use this as another example to help us understand God's nature. **Distribute three different-colored strings to each student.**

Write the titles "God the Father," "God the Son," and "God the Holy Spirit" on the board. Let's say each string represents one part of God's nature. Take the white strand. We can let it represent God the Father. Let's use some words from our previous lessons to describe Him. *(Holy; perfect; all-knowing; powerful.)* **Write these words on the board under**

the title "God the Father."

Now let's take the red strand and say it represents God the Son. Let's use some words from our previous lessons to describe Him. *(Loving; sacrificing; holy; powerful.)* **Write these words under the title "God the Son."**

Take the blue strand. Let's say it represents God the Holy Spirit. What are some words we learned that describe Him? *(Comforter; perfect; revealer; holy.)* **Write these under the title "God the Holy Spirit."**

Now take these three strands and weave or braid them together. **Instruct students to tie one end of their three strands together in a knot. Tape that end to a table or desk to make the braiding process easier. When the students finish braiding the cords, instruct them to tie the loose ends together to secure the braid. Give students time to complete their braids.**

Feel how strong the cord is. It is made up of three different strands, but it is one cord. That is the way God is. Look at our word lists under God the Father, God the Son, and God the Holy Spirit.

• What words are the same? *(Note the words that are the same.)*

• What words are different? *(Note the words that are different.)*

God is three Persons with three distinct characteristics, but He is still one God. Remember that we called this fact about God the Trinity. We will learn a little more about this in the Bible story today.

BIBLE STORY: Three in One

Before Class: Review the material on the Trinity from Lesson 1. To prepare your visuals, cut out each of the four Trinity Triangle drawings from the reproducibles. Also, cut a triangle from poster board that is the same size as a Trinity Triangle. (Use one of the triangles as a pattern when you cut.) Glue the triangle with the words onto the poster-board triangle.

Tape the bottom edge of each drawing to one side of the poster-board triangle. (See the diagram.)

Fold the pictures over to the back so that they are behind the center triangle. Fold them in order so that "God With Us" is on the bottom, "The Baptism of Jesus" is in the middle, and "Creation" is on top.

To begin your story, keep the pictures folded behind the poster-board triangle so students cannot see them. As you tell each part of the story, you will flip up that illustration. At the end of the Bible story time, all four triangles will make one large triangle shape. The Trinity Triangles will fit together so that the rope will intertwine to make a continuous strand around the triangle. You will be prompted when to do each action as you tell the story.

Make sure students have Bibles. Gather the students in a circle around you. Hold up the "God Is" diagram.

- Do you remember what the triangle represented when we first began studying about God and His character? *(The Trinity.)*

We learned that each Person of the Trinity has His own role to fill. Like the rope activity we did, we can say that God has three "strands," yet He is just one "rope." Although each strand is separate, the rope isn't complete without each strand. Although each Person of the Trinity is separate, God is not complete without each Person.

Hold up the poster-board triangle, but keep all three Trinity Triangle pictures hidden behind it. It might surprise you to learn that all three Persons of the Trinity have been involved in every important thing God has done. This shows us that God the Father, God the Son, and God the Holy Spirit never disagree about anything. They all work together to make things happen God's way. To show how this works, let's look at several events in the Bible that were very important milestones in history.

- What's the first thing the Bible mentions that God did? *(He created the world.)*

Read Genesis 1:1. Flip up the creation picture. God is so creative. He made things we can't even imagine. We are just learning about the many things that God made that we haven't discovered yet. Think about electricity. It has always been here, yet it has only been in the last few hundred years that scientists began learning about it. Not too long ago, scientists discovered tiny living things called bacteria. More recently, scientists have discovered even tinier living things called viruses. Both bacteria and viruses are so tiny that we can't see them without special equipment. God created things that are so tiny that people can't even see them.

Now think about the huge things God created. Who could measure the sun? Or get close enough to touch it? No one can. Who could put a mountain in his pocket? God could. God made the whole universe with just a word. Let's see just how God worked to create all these wondrous things.

Divide students into three groups. Assign each group one of the following references: Psalm 104:30; Nehemiah 9:6; Hebrews 1:2. Have each group discuss the question: "According to your verse, which Person of the Trinity was the Creator?"

Give groups a few moments to read and discuss. Then ask the above question of each group. Group 1 should answer "the Spirit of God," group 2 "God the Father," and group 3 "Jesus."

Did you realize that each Person in the Trinity participated in the creation of the universe? They were all in agreement. They each had their part. And look at what a marvelous, miraculous job they did!

Now let's look at another time when God showed Himself in three ways.

Flip up the second triangle picture. The baptism of Jesus was an important time in His life. He was starting His ministry, which would end with His death on the cross and His resurrection from the dead. How would the people know that Jesus was the true Savior of the world? He looked like a man. But He was also God.

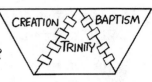

The first proof came when He was baptized. All three Persons of the Trinity came together to show that Jesus is the true Son of God. **Have groups read Matthew 3:13–16. Group 1 should decide what God the Father is doing in this story. Group 2 decides what Jesus is doing. Group 3 decides what the Holy Spirit is doing. Give groups a few moments to read and discuss. Have groups report on what their Person of the Trinity did during the baptism of Jesus.**

Can you see that here God is working in total agreement as three Persons? God shows that He is One but that He also has three roles to play.

Now let's turn to our own life. Do God the Father, God the Son, and God the Holy Spirit work together for us? Oh, yes they do! This is the exciting part for us. All three Persons of the Trinity work together to make sure that every believer gets to heaven.

Read 1 Peter 1:1,2. In this verse, God calls believers "the elect." That means that He chose us just as we choose someone for a game we're playing. Only when He chooses us, it's so much more important, and it's forever. He also says that we are strangers in the world. That means that our real home is in heaven, not here on earth. God has prepared for us a place so beautiful in heaven that when we see it, we'll wonder why we ever thought it was beautiful here on earth.

In these verses we can see the role of each Person of the Trinity in our salvation:

God the Father chose us ("the foreknowledge of God the Father").

Jesus died for us ("for obedience to Jesus Christ and sprinkling by His blood").

The Holy Spirit lives in us ("through the sanctifying work of the Spirit").

God chose us to be a member of His family before He even created the world. He knew you were going to become a Christian before you were born. Long before you were born, Jesus the Son came to earth to die for you to make it possible for you to live with God forever. When He went back to heaven, Jesus sent the Holy Spirit to live in you, to make your spirit holy like God is holy, to teach you to obey God's commands.

Flip up the third picture. Read 1 Peter 1:3–5. In these verses, God tells us that He will never let us miss making it to our home in heaven. His power keeps us safe. **Point out Jesus, the dove as the Spirit, and God the Father as the protecting hand in the picture.**

- How does it make you feel to know that God the Father, God the Son, and God the Holy Spirit all cooperate to make you a permanent member of God's family? *(Excited because I didn't think of it that way before. It shows me how much God loves me.)*

170

- How does knowing that the Trinity worked together in your salvation make you feel about God? *(It makes me love Him more. I want to thank Him.)*

The Trinity works together to make everything good happen. Do you see how these pictures fit together to make one shape, a triangle? Look how the three strands of rope all fit together around the triangle. That's how the Trinity works. It may seem that God is really three separate Persons. And He is. But all three Persons are also one God.

No human can explain exactly what the Trinity is like. Only God understands it completely. But we can trust God's Word when it tells us that God is three Persons in one.

CHECK FOR UNDERSTANDING: Tell It Again, Sam!

Have a volunteer briefly explain the roles of the Trinity in creation using the creation triangle. Have other volunteers do this with the other two triangles. Using the strands of rope from the Opening Activity, a fourth volunteer can explain how everything God does, He does as one. Then have a fifth volunteer explain the "God Is" diagram.

LESSON ACTIVITY: Three Prayer Strands

Just as we learned that the three Persons of the Trinity work together to accomplish God's will, the Trinity also plays another important part in our lives. All three Persons of the Trinity help us to pray. It's as if there are three strands wound together making sure our prayers get to God and that He hears them. That's what makes prayer especially strong. We learned about this in an earlier lesson. Let's see what you remember.

Have students reform their three groups. Give each group one of the following references: Matthew 6:6; John 14:13; Romans 8:26. Ask groups to figure out which verse provides the answers to the following questions. Write the questions on the chalkboard.

- **Who should we pray to?** *(God the Father—Matthew 6:6.)*

- **Whose name should we use to get our prayers answered?** *(Jesus—John 14:13.)*

- **Who helps us with the right words to say?** *(The Holy Spirit—Romans 8:26.)*

After a few moments, have groups report on which question is answered by their verse and which Person of the Trinity is associated with that question.

Isn't it amazing that each time you pray, all three Persons of the Trinity are involved? They all want you to pray. The Bible tells us that Jesus is in heaven right now, sitting at the right hand of His Father, helping us get our prayers answered.

Let's look at how this works by writing a prayer in class. **Draw a large rope with three strands on the board. (See diagram.) Also write out the prayer as you talk about it during the discussion time.**

- How will we start our prayer? Do we address our prayer to someone? *(God the Father.)*

Label the first rope strand "God listens for our prayers." The Father is in heaven, waiting for you to talk to Him. He is the One who will answer your prayer. **To begin your written prayer, write "Dear God" on the board.**

- How will we end our prayer? Do you know what God wants us to say when we close our prayer? *(In Jesus' name.)*

God wants us to pray in Jesus' name because He is the Person who is responsible for getting our prayers through to God. **Label the second strand "We ask in Jesus' name."** If Jesus hadn't died on the cross to pay for our sins, our sins would block our prayers from getting to God. Now Jesus is sitting right next to the Father, making sure that we can come before God's throne in prayer any time we want. All we need to do is confess what we've done wrong and God will listen. **Write "In Jesus' name" below "Dear God," leaving space to write the prayer between the two parts.**

- Who helps us with our praying? *(The Holy Spirit.)*

Our prayers would not be acceptable to God if the Holy Spirit didn't help us. **Label the third strand "Holy Spirit helps us pray."** He tells the Father what we need or want even when we don't have the words to explain it.

Between the two parts of the prayer, write: "Holy Spirit, help me pray with a clean heart."

Now we can add whatever we need to our prayer. We might want to add a few thank-yous and praises to God. **Discuss with the students about what to put in the prayer. Review the ACTS plan and write the students' suggestions for each part.** A—We can tell God how much we love Him. C—We can tell God how sorry we are for the sins we have done. T—We can thank God for helping us. S—We can pray for others. **Ask students to suggest prayer requests for others, such as "Help my neighbor who is old," or "Guide my pastor as he preaches today."**

APPLICATION: A Prayer With Three Strands

Distribute paper and pencils. Today, I want you to write out a prayer to God. **It may be just a couple of sentences long.** In your prayer, use the three strands of prayer that we talked about: praying to God the Father, praying in Jesus' name, and asking the Holy Spirit to help me pray. Refer to them on the board.

- What do you need to talk to God about right now? *(Allow students to respond. Make sure each student has something he or she wants to pray about.)*

Give students time to write their prayers. Circulate among the students to help those who are having difficulties. When students finish writing, spend a few moments in silence to allow students to talk to God using their prayer.

MEMORY VERSE ACTIVITY: Trinity Triangles

 Before Class: Cut out a large triangle from poster board. With a marker, divide the large triangle into three equal triangles. Write each verse part on one of the smaller triangles as follows: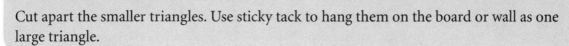

> *May the grace of the Lord Jesus Christ,*
> *and the love of God,*
> *and the fellowship of the Holy Spirit be with you all (2 Corinthians 13:14).*

Cut apart the smaller triangles. Use sticky tack to hang them on the board or wall as one large triangle.

Our verse today comes from 2 Corinthians 13:14. This was Paul's final statement to the church at Corinth. Let's read the verse together. **Read the verse.**

- What three persons are included in the verse? *(Jesus Christ; God; and the Holy Spirit.)*

I have written the verse on three smaller triangles that make one large triangle. This reminds us that the three persons of God are called the Trinity. **Read the verse together several more times. Have a student take away one part of the verse by removing one of the smaller triangles. Say the verse. Put the missing piece back and ask another student to take away another piece. Say the verse. Do this several times until you feel students are familiar with the verse. Have the students divide into pairs and practice the verse together.**

Optional Activity: Draw a triangle on a sheet of paper. With a marker, divide it into three smaller triangles. Make a photocopy of the triangle for each student. During the activity, instruct students to write the memory verse on the triangle in three parts, just like the verse is written on the large poster-board triangle. Have students form pairs. Have pairs cut apart the smaller triangles and practice saying the verse by removing one small triangle at a time.

Reconvene as a class and recite the verse again.

WEEKLY ASSIGNMENT: Using the Strands of Prayer

Have students take out their braided cords, untie the knot at one end, and untwist them. Do not untie the other knot.

This week, use your strands of yarn to help you remember to pray. Let each strand represent one Person in the Trinity: God the Father, Jesus the Son, or God the Holy Spirit. Tack this "rope" to your bulletin board or tape it to your bedroom wall. Each day, spend a few moments in prayer. Make sure you pray to the Father, ask the Holy Spirit's help, and close your prayer in Jesus' name. To show that the Trinity is involved in the prayer you prayed, braid one twist with your three strands. Clip the twist with a paper clip to keep it from unraveling. **Hand out paper clips.**

See if you can pray enough times to braid your three strands all the way to the bottom. Then you might want to get three different colors of string or yarn and try it again.

Close in prayer, using the three strands of prayer, asking God to bless your students as they keep walking with God and obeying what they have learned through the three units of *Discovering Our Awesome God*.

Trinity Triangle—Creation

Trinity Triangle–
The Baptism of Jesus

Trinity Triangle—
God With Us

Trinity Triangle

TRINITY
GOD THE FATHER
GOD THE SON
GOD THE HOLY SPIRIT

The Story of Jesus

The video *The Story of Jesus for Children* is designed to show children of all ages the true story of Jesus as adapted from the Gospel of Luke. The video will introduce your students to the life of Jesus through a format that they understand well—moving pictures and sound.

Most of the video scenes were taken from the adult film version of *JESUS*, which has introduced millions of people to our Savior. The *JESUS* film has been shown on every major continent of the world, has been translated into 638 languages, and is being used by thousands of missions and church groups around the world. This children's version of the video is an effective way to introduce your students to the life, ministry, death, and resurrection of Jesus.

You may wish to show this video before you begin your Children's Discipleship Series lessons. During the first unit in the series, "Who Is Jesus?," your students will learn about who Jesus is and what He has done for us. The video can serve as a dynamic introduction to the lesson material as well as an evangelistic tool for those students who have never received Jesus as their Savior. Units 2 and 3 build on this introduction to Jesus by showing your students how to begin their Christian adventure.

The video is 62 minutes long. If your class periods are one hour or less, you may choose to show the video over two sessions. The following chart gives two lesson plans you can use to fit the program you are offering for your students.

NUMBER OF SESSIONS	TIME NEEDED	LESSON PLAN
1	70 to 90 minutes	• Introduce the video • View the entire video • Allow for response from the video
2	45 to 60 minutes	• Introduce the video • View the video up to the events of the crucifixion • View the rest of the video • Allow for response from the video

Note: To fit this study into a yearly quarter of 13 lessons, begin with the single-lesson video presentation and omit Lesson 13 (the review lesson).

Lesson Materials

To view the video, you will need to obtain the following:

- A copy of the video *The Story of Jesus for Children* (See Resources to order.)

- A VCR/TV

- A copy of the booklet *The Greatest Promise* for each student (See Resources to order.)

- A copy of a Promise Card for each student (A reproducible page is provided at the end of this lesson.)

- Pencils

Lesson Objectives

As you prepare for the video lesson, keep in mind the following lesson objectives:

- To show students the true story of Jesus

- To allow students to see and understand the promises of God through His Son Jesus

- To give every student who views the video an opportunity to voluntarily choose to ask Jesus to live in them

LESSON PLAN

OPENING ACTIVITY: Introduce the Video

 Before Class: Cue the video. Gather your students around the TV. To begin, give the following brief history of the video.

About 2,000 years ago, Jesus of Nazareth was born in Bethlehem. He was God's Son sent to earth. He said, "If you have seen Me, you know what God is like." He also said, "I have come to do God's will on earth." Because He is God, what He said and how He lived and died is the most important story we'll ever hear. How Jesus lived and what He taught is the standard we must use to measure right from wrong.

The video we will see is called *The Story of Jesus for Children.* Some of you may have seen parts of this video in your church or school or perhaps even on television. Let me give you some facts about the video.

1. Scenes from the original film were done in the nation of Israel as close as possible to where the original events took place 2,000 years ago.

2. Dozens of experts such as historians, archaeologists, and theologians worked for five years doing research to make sure the film was accurate.

3. In the video, Jesus speaks only the words recorded in the Gospel of Luke from God's book, the Bible.

The children in this video are actors. The parts they play are only a story. The children's story is not found in the Bible. The reason the video presents a children's story along with the story of Jesus is to help you understand what is happening. We do not know how children interacted with Jesus while He was on earth. We do know that Jesus loved children very much. But the facts about Jesus and what He did and said are true. The children's story may have happened something like this . . .

LESSON ACTIVITY: Show the Video

Show the video all the way to the end. The video is not over after the last dramatic scene. The last part of the video gives your students an opportunity to invite Jesus to live in them.

APPLICATION: Allow for Responses

When the video is finished, hand out the Promise Cards and pencils. Say: Please write your name, address, and telephone number on the Promise Card. Then check the boxes to tell your ideas about what you have said, thought, or done as you watched the video.

Distribute *The Greatest Promise* booklets when appropriate. This booklet is yours to take home and read with your family and friends. If you have made a decision to invite Jesus into your life, come and tell me after I dismiss our class.

Close in prayer, thanking God for sending Jesus to die for us. You may want to introduce the unit on Jesus before you dismiss your students.

Collect the cards and quickly note the boxes each student checked. Make yourself available to talk to students who indicated that they asked Jesus to come into their lives. Read through *The Greatest Promise* booklet with students who have questions about their relationship with God. You may want to ask other adults who are experienced children's teachers to help you with this counseling.

Promise Card
(Commitment Card)

☐ I prayed today and asked Jesus to live in me.

☐ I already asked Jesus to live in me.

☐ I am not ready to ask Jesus into my life.

☐ I would like to learn more about Jesus.

NAME: _____

ADDRESS: _____

_____

CITY: _____

STATE: _____ ZIP: _____

☐ BOY ☐ GIRL AGE: _____

PHONE: _____

Give to your teacher or parent.

Promise Card
(Commitment Card)

☐ I prayed today and asked Jesus to live in me.

☐ I already asked Jesus to live in me.

☐ I am not ready to ask Jesus into my life.

☐ I would like to learn more about Jesus.

NAME: _____

ADDRESS: _____

_____

CITY: _____

STATE: _____ ZIP: _____

☐ BOY ☐ GIRL AGE: _____

PHONE: _____

Give to your teacher or parent.

My Prayer

Today I prayed this prayer:

Dear God,

I believe Jesus is Your Son. Thank You that Jesus died on the cross for all the wrong things I have thought and said and done. Please forgive me for my sins. I ask Jesus to be with me and to live in me always. Help me to be the kind of person You want me to be. Thank You for answering my prayer. Amen.

NAME: _____

DATE: _____

Keep in your Bible.

My Prayer

Today I prayed this prayer:

Dear God,

I believe Jesus is Your Son. Thank You that Jesus died on the cross for all the wrong things I have thought and said and done. Please forgive me for my sins. I ask Jesus to be with me and to live in me always. Help me to be the kind of person You want me to be. Thank You for answering my prayer. Amen.

NAME: _____

DATE: _____

Keep in your Bible.

Jesus and Me Every Day

When you ask Jesus to forgive you and invite Him to be with you, He really is with you now and always. He always keeps His promises. In the Bible Jesus makes many promises to help you be certain about your relationship with Him. Here are two of His promises:

"I am with you always." *(Matthew 28:20)*
"I will never leave you." *(Hebrews 13:5)*

As you begin this new life with God and His Son, Jesus, God will help you make the right choices. Here is another promise from God's book, the Bible:

"God is working in you to help you want to do what pleases Him. Then He gives you the power to do it." *(Philippians 2:13)*

(Bible verses from *International Children's Bible*)

Jesus and Me Every Day

When you ask Jesus to forgive you and invite Him to be with you, He really is with you now and always. He always keeps His promises. In the Bible Jesus makes many promises to help you be certain about your relationship with Him. Here are two of His promises:

"I am with you always." *(Matthew 28:20)*
"I will never leave you." *(Hebrews 13:5)*

As you begin this new life with God and His Son, Jesus, God will help you make the right choices. Here is another promise from God's book, the Bible:

"God is working in you to help you want to do what pleases Him. Then He gives you the power to do it." *(Philippians 2:13)*

(Bible verses from *International Children's Bible*)

Names of God

God is called by many wonderful names in the Bible. These names hold an important key to understanding who He is and how He cares for His people. (The names in parentheses are God's names as written in the original language of the Bible, Hebrew.) God's names tell us about His nature, character, and never-changing relationship to His people.

The following chart includes ways to help you understand how wonderful God is. Look up two or more of the verses. Write down some facts about what the verses say about God's name. Then write some ideas of what that name means to you, His promises to you, and how God will help you.

GOD'S NAME	BIBLE VERSES TO LOOK UP	WHAT DO THE VERSES SAY ABOUT GOD'S NAME?	HOW DOES THIS NAME HELP YOU UNDERSTAND GOD?
Lord or Master (*Adonai*)	Psalm 39:7; 54:4; 71:5; 73:28; 86:5; 86:12; 86:15; 140:7; Isaiah 6:8; Ezekiel 18:25; Luke 6:46		
God (*El*)	Psalm 22; Mark 15:34		
The Strong, Faithful One; the only true God (*Elohim*)	Genesis 1:26		
The Exalted One; the Most High God (*El-Elyon*)	Numbers 24:16; 2 Samuel 22:14; Psalm 18:13; Isaiah 14:12–15; Daniel 7:27		
The Everlasting God (*El-Olam*)	Genesis 9:16; Exodus 40:15; Deuteronomy 33:27; Proverbs 10:25; 45:17; Jeremiah 31:3; Daniel 4:3; Habakkuk 3:6; John 3:16; 2 Thessalonians 1:8,9; Hebrews 5:9		

God's Name	Bible Verses to Look Up	What do the Verses Say About God's Name?	How Does This Name Help You Understand God?
The God Who Sees (*El-Roi*)	Psalm 139:1,2,7; John 5:19		
The Almighty God (*El-Shaddai*)	Genesis 17:1,2; Exodus 6:3; Job 40:2		
God With Us (*Immanuel*)	Matthew 1:23; Galatians 4:4,5		
I AM (*Jehovah, Yahweh*)	Exodus 3:14,15; John 4:25,26; 8:12, 8:28; 10:9,11,36; 15:1; James 1:17; Hebrews 13:8		
The Lord our Provider (*Jehovah-Jireh*)	Genesis 22:8,14; Hebrews 22:17–19		
The Lord Who Sanctifies or Purifies (*Jehovah-Mekaddesh*)	Exodus 13:2; Leviticus 19:2; 1 Samuel 2:2; Psalm 103:1; Proverbs 9:10; Isaiah 6:3; John 17:17; Romans 12:1; 1 Peter 1:15,16		
The Lord our Banner or Victory (*Jehovah-Nissi*)	Exodus 14:13; 17:15, 16; Deuteronomy 20:3, 4; Isaiah 13:2–4,11; John 3:14; 16:33; 1 Corinthians 15:57; Ephesians 2:8,9; 6:10–12		
The Lord our Shepherd (*Jehovah-Rohi*)	Isaiah 40:10,11; Ezekiel 34:11–16; Psalm 23:1,4; 139:2; John 10:11; Hebrews 13:20; 1 Peter 2:25		
God our Healer (*Jehovah-Rophe*)	Numbers 12:13; Psalm 103:2,3; Jeremiah 3:22; Malachi 4:2; Matthew 4:23; Luke 4:18; John 5:36; Revelation 22:17		
The Captain of our Salvation (*Jehovah-Sabaoth*)	1 Samuel 1:3; Jeremiah 11:20; Zechariah 4:6		

GOD'S NAME	BIBLE VERSES TO LOOK UP	WHAT DO THE VERSES SAY ABOUT GOD'S NAME?	HOW DOES THIS NAME HELP YOU UNDERSTAND GOD?
The Lord our Peace (*Jehovah-Shalom*)	Numbers 6:24–26; Judges 6:13,23,24; Isaiah 9:6; 26:2–4,12; Matthew 11:28,29; John 14:27; Romans 5:1; Philippians 4:5–7; Colossians 1:20		
The Lord Is There (*Jehovah-Shammah*)	Exodus 33:14–16; Psalm 132:8; Isaiah 63:9; Ezekiel 43:1–7; Matthew 28:20; John 1:14; 1 Corinthians 3:16; Ephesians 2:19–22		
The Lord our Righteousness (*Jehovah-Tsidkenu*)	Deuteronomy 32:4; Psalm 89:14; Jeremiah 23:5,6; Daniel 9:7,8; Acts 3:14; Romans 3:20; 1 Corinthians 1:30; 2 Corinthians 5:21		

Resources

"THE STORY OF JESUS FOR CHILDREN" VIDEO

This 62-minute video entertains, educates, and introduces children to the life of Jesus of Nazareth, giving them a chance to see and hear the whole story of Jesus at once! The video answers questions in clear and concrete terms, provides fast action, and ends with an invitation, by a child to children, to choose to invite Jesus into their lives. Children of all ages will enjoy this captivating retelling of the true story of Jesus from a child's perspective.

THE GREATEST PROMISE

The Greatest Promise booklet is developed especially for children. Complete with Scripture references, illustrations from the *JESUS* film, and more. This is a great follow-up tool for use after the video. One copy of *The Greatest Promise* booklet comes free with every *The Story of Jesus for Children* video.

To order additional copies, contact The JESUS Film Project at 800-432-1997.

RESURRECTION EGGS: THE EASTER STORY FOR CHILDREN
Randall Lee Walti

Twelve colorful eggs contain symbols that illustrate events in the death, burial, and resurrection of Jesus. An easy-to-understand booklet explains how to use these Resurrection Eggs®, and Bible stories reveal the significance of each object.

To order, contact FamilyLife at 800-FL-TODAY or visit www.familylife.com.

WOULD YOU LIKE TO BELONG TO GOD'S FAMILY?
Bill Bright
(ISBN 1-56399-081-4)

The popular and practical *Four Spiritual Laws* is now available in a fun, illustrated format kids can read and understand. Designed for elementary-aged children, *Would You Like to Belong to God's Family?* presents the gospel as four facts (rather than four laws) to help them learn how to become members of God's family through faith in Jesus Christ.

THE GOOD NEWS COMIC
Bill Bright
(ISBN 1-56399-094-6)

Help children understand who God is in a simple and relevant way with this fun, colorful gospel story in comic book form—a favorite children's ministry tool for decades! Ideal for Sunday school and vacation Bible school, or as bag stuffers for Halloween or birthday parties.

THE GOOD NEWS GLOVE

Bill Bright

(ISBN 1-56399-074-1)

A classic and fun witnessing tool, this colorful glove helps children understand and remember the gospel. Each finger communicates a basic spiritual truth in an exciting, game-like fashion that captures kids' attention and hearts. Use it alone or with *The Good News Comic.*

IN SEARCH OF THE GREATEST TREASURE

Bill Bright

(ISBN 1-56399-120-9)

Join a delightful band of children as they embark on a treasure hunt…not for buried treasure, but for the greatest person who ever lived. Written in comic-book fashion, this brightly-colored, easy-to-use booklet helps children understand who Jesus is and why He is the Greatest Treasure.

A CHILD OF THE KING

Bill Bright and Marion R. Wells

(ISBN 1-56399-150-0)

A Child of the King is a timeless tale of a kingdom turned away from the sun, a brave but vulnerable orphan, a diabolical foe and a king whose love never ends. The story could be your own. Perhaps it is.

Written in the beloved, allegorical tradition of C. S. Lewis' *Chronicles of Narnia* and J. R. R. Tolkien's *The Lord of the Rings, A Child of the King* takes you on a quest for truth, virtue, and self-worth in a dark and hostile world. Share the adventures of Jotham, the People of the Book, and others in the Kingdom of Withershins…and realize your own high calling as a child of the King.

HAVE YOU MADE THE WONDERFUL DISCOVERY OF THE SPIRIT-FILLED LIFE?

Bill Bright

(ISBN 1-56399-020-2)

Discover the reality of the Spirit-filled life and how to live in moment-by-moment dependence on Him. Millions have learned to live the abundant life that Christ promises by following the simple, biblical truths found in this booklet. Use the booklet to refresh your own walk with Christ or to share with others.

These and other fine products from *NewLife* Publications are available from your favorite bookseller or by calling (800) 235-7255 (within U.S.) or (407) 826-2145, or by visiting www.newlifepubs.com.

Certificate

This certificate is awarded to:

for successfully completing "Discovering Our Awesome God," Book 2 of the Children's Discipleship Series

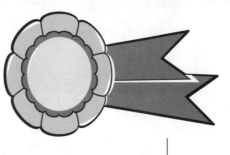

CHURCH AND CITY

DATE

NAME, POSITION

NAME, POSITION